No More Kisses for Me

by Gayle Hiller

ISBN: 978-1-7358118-3-3

Unbound Publishing is committed to publishing works of quality and integrity. In that spirit, we are proud to offer this book to our readers; however, the story, the experiences, and the words are the author's alone. Some individuals mentioned in the book may have different memories, as they experienced this story from another point of view. The conversations in the book all come from the author's recollections, though they are not written to represent word-for-word transcripts. Rather, the author has retold them in a way that evokes the feeling and meaning what was said and in all instances, the essence of the dialogue is accurate.

Contents

Acknowledgments .7
Dedications 9
Preface. 13
Letter 1: The Start 19
Letter 2 29
Letter 3 45
Letter 4 57
Letter 5 69
Letter 6 77
Letter 7 85
Letter 8 101
Letter 9 111
Letter 10. 127
Letter 11 137
Letter 12. 147
Letter 13. 161
Letter 14. 167
Letter 15. 183
Letter 16. 189
Letter 17. 199
Letter 18: Closure. 207
About the Author 213
About the Publisher 215

Acknowledgments

I would like to thank my cousins Caroline and David Stevens for their constant love and support and without them these letters would never have been written.

Thanks to my Mummy Norma Hiller for always being there for me and the family and a big thanks to Max her partner for all the things you do for us.

My friend and Neighbour Carol Temple who has been by my side through ups and downs.

Special Thanks to Beverly and Rick Mayston of Agent Fox Media and Jerry Mooney and Troy Lambert of Unbound Publishing for believing in me and guiding me through which led to this wonderful opportunity, so that you can hear my Story.

Thank you Mick Mamuzelos for your wonderful artwork

Thank you to my late Aunt and Uncle Eva and Benny Hall, they gave me a normal family life when I was a child and a teenager, living with them were some of the best days of my life they showed me what real family love is and Eric Hall for his constant support.

Dedications

It was late at night on the balcony of my cousin's apartment in Spain where I learned that I had written my father 17 letters containing nearly 43,000 words. I felt really pleased with myself that through the depression and heartache, I had managed to write down exactly how I felt about him and use words that I had never been able to when he was alive. I lived in fear of him shouting at me and telling me to Shhh... like I knew nothing, once again making me feel worthless.

It was my cousin, Caroline, who suggested I write my father a letter, so every morning I was able, I sat alone in the coffee shop in a corner and set to work on writing. I soon found that one letter became two, two became four, four became eight and on and on.... I had written all the letters on my mobile phone. Through the grieving, the heartache and especially the tears, writing my feelings down really helped me deal with my grief. I felt so proud of what I had achieved.

Writing these letters to my father has been a long healing process. I have had to face the truth and battle on through the pain. Of course, this book would never have come to fruition if it were not for my cousin Caroline, who encouraged me to write my father a letter to help me "get everything off my chest" as they say.

I want to say a huge heartfelt thank you to her and her husband David for helping me through the grieving process. They were my counsellors and many a time was spent in their home in Spain crying, but we laughed, too. Going to see them was my sanctuary. They are my two favourite people.

This book is dedicated to my Mother. We do not get the opportunity to rewrite the past but through maturity and hindsight I came to realise our hurt and experience was not dissimilar. We have had a turbulent relationship over the years, but I thank you for all you have done for me and my children. I don't think I ever told you how much I love and admire you for your strength. I don't know how you could have ever gotten over your husband / my father for walking out on you after many years of marriage, and after you and your family financially supported his dream. Then when he achieved his dream, he became a nightmare. Did I tell you how much I love you? xx

I also dedicate this book to my late Auntie Eva who always believed in me and fought in my corner. She was the most wonderful woman and living at her home with my Late Uncle Benny, which I did on a regular basis as a child, showed me what a loving family was. I wanted to stay with them forever.

And finally, my daughters Jade and Amber and their wonderful partners. To my son Tyrone and my grandson Harvey. I love you all with all my heart. I am so proud of you all. When I look at you, I know that I did something very right.

Gayle Hiller

Preface

Flung at 30 mph in the air after being hit when crossing the road from school my body and skull smashed against an iron streetlamp and slumped at full force onto the concrete road, I lay unconscious. Fighting in hospital in a coma for my life, my nightmares had just begun. A year later, while learning to write and walk again, my father walked out on his family. A part of me died then and has haunted me every minute of the day. The blood from cutting my wrists mixed with the water as it swirled around the blue sink. A desperate attempt to see him.

The successful father who loved the adulation of his peers, I was treated as a nuisance. I felt abandoned and tried to get back my father's love and attention for 40 years. Our lack of a normal father daughter relationship scarred me deeply. I had all the typical signs one displays when a father/daughter relationship goes bad: I fought depression, self-harm, and self- loathing because everything I had done in my life was wrong in his eyes.

To make himself feel better he bragged to his family what a wonderful father he was when in fact it distracted from the truth. He was an absent father and only came in and out of my life when it suited him or for his own gain.

He never realised the devastation it caused. That yearning for my Daddy caused a severe sadness and pain that I still carry with me today.

On the odd occasion when I attended a family party, he would make an entrance with his new wife and all the family smiled and spoke to them. I was not included and left to feel like a stranger. It left me engulfed in that familiar state of sadness and loss, although I had grieved for him a thousand times throughout my life.

Two short lived marriages and bringing up three children as a single mother only reminded me that I was a failure in his eyes. In fact, he never commented on how well I bought up three polite, well rounded children and a grandson in the former years.

My father passed away in 2018. I was unable to grieve, and took pills to sedate me, to numb me from any emotion I was feeling. I had spent nearly all my life trying to rebuild a relationship with him, almost like being in a battle. But when he died the battle was over. In some strange way it was also a huge relief, after fighting all my life for his approval and respect I suddenly realised, "I don't have to do that anymore." I had closure.

In fact, now I am receiving praise and admiration from others for who I really am. I was in the newspapers for accidentally discovering I could paint on canvas while doing arts and crafts with my grandson. A well-known grime artist was alerted to my painting with the Director of his Music video that was being filmed in the council estate next to the community centre. My painting was on display there, and I was called in to sign the painting for the grime artist, Stormzy.

Despite everything I have had to endure in my life I have found myself in a place where I am appreciated for my talent without any help from my father.

It's been an extremely long hard journey to get to this point, from an innocent child who craved the attention from my father and also his second wife who was always opinionated towards me. They both saw me as an inconvenience.

I bared my soul whilst writing these letters. It helped me, and I hope it helps others.

My father was Tony Hiller, co-writer of the biggest selling Eurovision winning song. 'Save your Kisses for Me.' It was sung by The Brotherhood of man. The two Male singers Martin Lee and Lee Sheridan also co-wrote it. The song was a hit in 40 different countries. They were the first Eurovision group to have a dance routine and set the precedence for the wonderful Eurovision song contest you see today.

My father was also a successful songwriter who wrote over 2,000 songs in his career. One of his other biggest hits by the first original Brotherhood of Man group was the song "United We Stand," co-written with Johnny Goodison who was a member of the original group.

It was in the charts for 15 weeks and a hit in other countries.

It was recorded by over 100 singers. It was used by United airlines for their advertising campaign and recently the spiritual anthem of 9/11. It was also used as a song for gay rights.

My father died 28 August 2018. I was unable to grieve and was in a bad way. Antidepressants helped the tsunami of grief that just appeared out of nowhere and whirled violently inside. Grief is one of the hardest things to deal with. I had suicidal thoughts and it brought up my past with my father. He walked out on us once and when he met his second wife. That was to be the demise of our relationship and I was cast aside. I have had to fight for his attention every day of my life since.

She never wanted me and my children in his life. As soon as I went to stay abroad, she got her foot into his mews house and his life. She threw away my bed and expensive designer scarves, bags and perfumes. What child has to plead for their father's time and attention? The hurtful and vindictive comments from them both, only seeing me once a month both told me I was no longer important in My Daddy's life. While they enjoyed the glitzy show business parties, the Rolls Royce's and rich life that I was once a part of and lived in a property worth millions of pounds.I was struggling as a single mother of 3 children. This was a far cry from my teenage years when I took breakfast at The Dorchester Hotel before I went to work as a receptionist in Radio Luxembourg and attended show-business parties and danced in top nightclubs.

I struggled with self-confidence and various issues which turned into depression. I used to self-diagnose my heartache and lack of self-worth with pills that I became addicted to. This book is multifaceted and shows the real Tony Hiller and the way my children and I were treated with total disregard. It touches on mental illness and me, his broken daughter, who was recuperating from a car accident and a major head injury when he walked out on us.

My father, Tony Hiller, always pushed me down, and when he saw that I was trying to get up again he just kept right on pushing me down again and again till I was eventually broken.

It was his way of controlling me. Maybe it was because the other woman in is life, SHE, controlled him.

He may have written 'Save Your Kisses for Me,' but I soon found out there were to be **No more kisses for me.**

By Gayle Hiller

Letter 1: The Start

Dear Daddy,

It has been 11 months since you passed away. Thank goodness I am functioning like a normal person now. Only a few months ago, I was literally drowning in my own tears, I was depressed, and at times felt suicidal. Thank goodness my children kept me going. Your grandchildren that you only saw, like me, every 4 to 6 weeks.

I cried for you, the daddy. I grew up with. I put you way up high on a pedestal because I was in love with Tony Hiller, the successful songwriter/record producer like everyone else. You had such charisma and loved being the entertainer. When I think about it, I don't remember a single evening we spent together as a family in our house, but I do remember the restaurants we frequented and the visits to your sisters' homes.

I also sobbed my heart out for all the years you kept me away from your life. You made me feel like I was a stranger, a nobody, certainly not your daughter. You just didn't want me and my children in you and your second wife's life. I can never forgive you for breaking my heart, never inviting the children and me over. When you had relatives from other countries at your home, but you invited my brother and his wife. Was that because of her? You spent all your time with her family when they were over from Australia. You put everyone first, ahead of your own daughter.

Do you have any idea of the hurt and damage you did to me? Do you?

When I went into Mummy's house a few months ago bawling my eyes out, she told me not to shed a tear for you, as you didn't deserve my tears.

"Dont waste any tears over that bastard, " she said.

The Mummy I gave a hard time to, because from a child you told me she was mad. I let you brainwash me against my own Mother. The tears well up in my eyes when I think how many times I argued with her and pushed her away. Thank goodness we are able to make amends; I would never have forgiven myself otherwise.

Mummy was right to say that, but bereavement doesn't discriminate. You can be fine one moment and from nowhere, a whirling hurricane enters your body and violently mixes up your heart and soul. You sob, uncontrollably, the saddest heartfelt tears.

Call me a coward, but I couldn't go through this. I opted for pills that sedated me, but tears still escaped my eyes and slid down my face.

Your family was all estranged from me and chose to comfort the black widow. I will never, ever forget the way they all made me and my children feel in your flat, your home, and this was all your fault. You didn't include us in anything and let your second wife be rude and disrespectful to us. You fed her narcissistic ego until she believed she was above everyone else. Butter wouldn't melt in her mouth, but the truth was, she was a recovering alcoholic. I have every respect for people who beat their addiction, but she shouldn't have looked down on my life when I know, for a fact, she wouldn't be able to cope with it.

I stood in the kitchen with these thoughts. I managed to rescue two aubergines l had placed on top of the shiny red apples that were placed in the colourful large pottery bowl. The vibrant light blue, orange, and yellow colours stood out and matched my mood. The back door was ajar, opening out to the garden. I like the garden to look natural, and don't have any flowers, just large green bushes. The garden fence that was battered when we had hurricane winds last year was put together by my son-in-law. I started painting the fence, but the paint was cheap (the only one I could afford) and didn't even cover the wood after two coats.

I cannot tell you what progress it is to actually want to cook. To feel motivated instead of curling up on the settee and dozing intermittently. The back door was my gateway to heaven, and as I fried the thin slices of aubergine with the very thin green chilies in the hot oil I began to shout out my grievances to you. There is so much I wanted to tell you when you were alive but was unable to.

Do you hear me now, Daddy? Have I got your time now? I don't think, however, you would be watching over me and your grandkids and great-grandson. After all, you never cared about us when you were alive, only in your own selfish, minimal way.

There was another family party this weekend, and the children and I weren't invited again. According to one of my cousins, someone from your family said I wasn't invited because I was a troublemaker. Really? I was snubbed at your Shiva / wake and told everyone the truth about how I felt, and they call me a troublemaker? Mind you, you never liked it when I expressed my opinions. It is so sad that certain members of your family speak about everyone behind their backs. People are so full of lies and deceit that they can't take the truth. The truth scares them and the person who speaks the truth even more.

Has anyone in your family bothered to call me and ask how the children and I are coping? But, then did you? You didn't even know what was going on in my life. You hadn't visited us for absolute years.

Do you remember when there were family weddings, parties etc.? Most of the time, I never went as I couldn't afford a cash present, and to buy me and my three children evening outfits would have cost a fortune. I sometimes used to hint that we didn't have anything appropriate to wear. You used to tell me that I couldn't go then. It might cramp your style.

If, on the odd occasion, I did go, I used to ask if you could write on the card from me and the children too. I found that embarrassing, but at big functions you had to give big money that I never had. Whenever I sign a card, I always put from me and the children. I suppose it was abnormal for her. You signed most of my birthday cards from Tony and her. Isn't that how you and she signed your cards to everyone? Were you incapable of signing them yourself? In order to be a parent, one must be absolutely selfless. Most people are too selfish to have children. You were too busy with your showbusiness life. It was obviously more important than having me.

I never understood why when there were just the two of you living in your garden flat that you needed two cleaners?

I remember your huge marble table that stood in front of your TV. You always had lots of things piled on it, including an orchid plant. She loved plants, didn't she? In fact, the Victorian small steps down to your basement flat were hard enough to navigate. Then we had to fight our way through the huge, overgrown plants she put in front of the front door. When the children and I visited once a month, we would always bring something like flowers or chocolates because we were just visitors and not treated like family.

What happened to the orchids we bought her? We never saw them again, very strange. Any birthday gift we bought her was never, ever seen again, so I didn't bother getting anything the last couple of years.

We were so unappreciated by her. I refer to her as she, because she never played a part in our lives. She didn't want to be called Nanny, grandma, or any name, so she is just she.

A pronoun, a naming word, nothing special. You would not imagine that some ordinary person with no redeeming qualities or personality could do such damage. The whole family runs around her, like the grieving widow, because it was just you and her, that is what she wanted, and you went along just to please her. So, I cannot expect the extended family to love and embrace me when my own Daddy saw me as a nuisance.

Do you remember Daddy, before her, when I said I was going to live abroad you begged me to stay? You promised to find me a place to live. Being young and curious, I wanted to start a new chapter in my life. iIn hindsight I should never have gone. Once I was out of the way, she got her foot in the door.

You never cared whether I was there or not at family functions. Why would any of them even try to bother with me now? No one invites me and my children preferring to have her. I am the estranged daughter from your first marriage, but my brother is from that marriage, too.

Is it because he is a male and he and his wife don't have children? And when you invite them over, there are no children for her to consider? She probably thinks like that, but Daddy, they were your grand-children and great-grandson, whom you should have spent time with. A lot of people I have spoken to think it is disgusting too, but no, I am not giving you names. I don't have to do anything now. I don't carry that heartache anymore of fighting for your love. I was so preoccupied with getting back your love that I have wasted a lot of blood, sweat, and tears. I now feel that hurt, that yearning, desperation, disappoint-ment had been lifted from me. Those chains have been unlocked, and I am now free.

Was it worth it? Most definitely not. It mentally im-prisoned me, and no one should ever live for some-one else's approval and love. We are all unique and beautiful and should be true to ourselves and live life for who we truly are. A life of regrets is an unfulfilled life.

So, as I stand here at the kitchen door looking out on to the garden, I let out all my anger and frustration to you with such a great voice. Jade just came in and asked who was with me. I felt a fool when she said she heard me shouting, which I tried to deny. When one has a love affair that ends, it is really painful when it finishes, but this was a different kind of love.

I cannot understand why she felt so threatened by me. There are many different relationships and different kinds of love. A father's love for his daughter should be unconditional. Did she give you some ultimatum: it's me or her?

Jade started to tell me about her job interview, when she had finished telling me, she took the dog out for a walk. I made the yoghurt with chopped garlic and poured it over the dish. My ex showed me how to make it. It is a Turkish, Kurdish dish and absolutely delicious. Shame you never tasted any of my delicious food, ever. In fact, in the last 35 years, you never knew me at all.

You know Daddy, sometimes when I went to see you with two of my children and my grandson, I sometimes only had the money for the train fares for all of us to see you on our monthly visits. Going to your plush flat, next to all the hotels, was a different world, especially when we went out to eat. We could choose anything on the menu and have copious glasses of diet coke.

As an adult, you still didn't want me to have a glass of wine, even though you used to bring your own bottle if it was the Iranian restaurant and drink the whole thing. You never even blinked an eye when the bill came, and it was usually around £150 plus the £20 tip you gave the waiter.

I couldn't understand why you told me you didn't have money. What person can afford that, on one meal?

When the school photos are taken, I never quite understand why they cost a fortune, but grandparents are so happy to receive them. If it's anything like Mummy, she would always buy a new frame and display them. Some years I just couldn't afford them. I remember that one particular year, I thought it nice to purchase one for you, as you only had a few very old photos of your grandchildren that she displayed along with other people' photos. There were three of me, and I was so embarrassed as I looked terrible in them. I had asked her to remove them, and I told her I would replace them, but she said she couldn't? I knew you had so many people from show business in your flat, and I didn't want them to think your daughter looked like that.

Tyrone had just had his school photo taken, so I bought one for Mummy and one for you.

I remember going in the end room, which was meant as a bedroom, but again she had turned it into a study so no one could stay. You never had any of your grandchildren stay, ever. Let's face it, you weren't exactly a grandfather that did grandfatherly things. I remember you sitting by the computer facing me.

I proudly took your grandson's photo out of my handbag and as I presented it to you, I was not quite ready for your reaction.

You looked at the photograph of your grandson and held it in front of you and asked

"What do you want me to do with this?"

Really, Daddy? What grandparent says that?

I told you to "put it in a frame and display it."

You held it up in front of you and moved it in my direction as a gesture for me to take it back." Take it. I have no room for it." I told you that I had bought it, especially for you. "I don't want it," you said.

I had to repeat myself that I bought it, especially for you." I was absolutely gobsmacked.

I took the photo from you and put it back in my bag, not bearing to look at you.

Again, like all the other times, I just accepted your callous behaviour.

That was a very hurtful thing that you did.

Daddy, you weren't a family man at all. You only did things to make yourself look good to others, but I knew the truth. I got on the train and cried all the way until I reached my destination. I never understood why she always took so many photos of us at the beginning of your relationship. Maybe it was to pretend to you that she cared about us and was going to be a great stepmother? Well, she wasn't.

Love you, Daddy

RIP...

Letter 2

Dear Daddy,

I am upset for my children that she hasn't invited any of them to the flat. It has bothered me a great deal. We all tried to do the right thing. She doesn't have any contact with me, but I want you to know that we all tried. I did try to tell you what she was like when you were alive. She could do no wrong in your eyes. Let's be honest Daddy since when did you even listen to me?

Now you are dead. She doesn't have to pretend anymore that is evident. Did she really try even when you were alive, Daddy? The truth always transpires in the end. Her total dislike towards me could not be controlled on her part, so she has shut me out, not only that but my children too, your grandchildren. Do you think that is nice?

I have to deal with people not liking my family and me when we have done nothing wrong. It is not a good feeling. Plus, I am a very sensitive soul, and just as I think my depression/mood is under control, there are times when I feel really hurt by your family's complete disregard for us. Like we are not your flesh and blood. You did this, Daddy, you never ever fought in our corner.

Tony Hiller the successful Songwriter/Record Producer, who left every single thing to his second wife. You know how difficult life was and still is for me. You had the money and power to alleviate that for the children and me.

I have got to be brutally honest with you Daddy, this is really unheard of, and I was not surprised to know that you changed your will three years before you died, but you had a bit of dementia then. I did not think it possible that you could have done this.

When you were on your deathbed, surrounded by people from show business, all crammed into your bedroom, our eyes actually met for the first time, after Eric Hall had told you that he played the song that you always said you wrote for me on his radio show.

I wanted desperately to talk to you, but we were never alone: even though your voice was weak and was nearing the end. You laughed with your showbiz friends and then you started crying on and off.

Tell me Daddy, is there life on the other side? I wish you could give me a sign. I can imagine you up there smiling with all the show biz people that have passed over. You must be in your element. Bragging about all the songs you wrote, which were hits, especially bragging about the Eurovision Song Contest and 'Save your Kisses for me.' How are your family, have you even spared them some time now you're in Heaven? It must be so wonderful to be reunited with them. Please give a kiss to my Auntie Eva and Uncle Benny, I loved them so much…

As I told you on your deathbed, I loved you so much. You are probably the only man I ever truly loved and looked up to. I have never been able to have a successful relationship.

I blame you for that! I meet a new man, but I know that it is not going to last from the beginning, because my first and biggest love, you, had been cruelly snatched away from me. First, after my accident, when I was abused in the hospital, in a coma and nearly died, you walked out. I had to do dramatic things for you to come and see me. Love equals heartache. Love equals drama and loss. Love hurts and I can't handle it. Love is elusive to me.

I was abused, Daddy or at least that is what it felt like to me at the time. I was a young, petrified, confused child. I wasn't able to talk to anyone about my deepest nightmares, especially to you. I think I tried many times to explain to you later on in life, but you were quick to voice your opinion before I was even able to tell you the depths of my experience.

I remember the cold water and the rough way in which I had a bed wash. I still get anxiety attacks and recurring nightmares, as I remember being tied by a blanket to the chair, which was the same as a baby's highchair. The Sister in the ward was always shouting, and her shrill voice went right through me.

For days I lay on the bed, unable to move my body and didn't know why, but then Mummy told me that the woman on the next bed told her that they were injecting me. Maybe that was to restrain me from hurting myself, but nothing was ever explained to me. All I remember was being manhandled. Not one kind word or explanation was given to me. I remember once, I slid under the restrain of a sheet, I am not clear what it was, all I know is that it tied me to the chair, so I was unable to move.

Are you listening to me now, Daddy? I was in a living hell. I still get nightmares about being restrained not being able to move. I don't want to keep revisiting the time as I lay in the hospital bed locked into my body. If I shut my eyes and open them again, I hoped to be in a different place. I used to scream out for somebody to help me, but no words came out. Daddy you used to say, " When are you going to stop all this stupidity about not going in lifts?" It wasn't just a lift to me, Daddy. There are even some toilet doors that I can't lock because that feeling of being trapped haunts me, even to this day. Do you understand Daddy, that I was in a living hell?

I remember, after what seemed an eternity, I managed to slide under the restraint as it was loose that day. I saw the sister opposite walking down the ward with two Doctors, I assumed they were Doctors. I was screaming, "help" as I didn't want to be tied up to the chair anymore. I tried to walk towards them, but with every step I took, I felt something or someone was dragging me back. As an adult I realise, that was normal practice, to be restrained in the 70s and they probably had to do it to keep me safe, but as a petrified young girl, it felt like they were physically abusing me.

Now do you understand why I am claustrophobic? I have every reason to be.

I remember when 'she' was walking to Hyde Park, and I heard that story again, about when a bike knocked her over, and she got a concussion. She told me it was just like my accident. Well, being knocked down by a bike, falling on to grass in a park as opposes to having a car smash into your body at over 30 miles an hour and being flung high into the air and your body and head smashed against an iron lamppost and then landing on the concrete pavement, is in no way the same thing.

Again, I have had to deal with yet, another problem alone, with no help from you. You set the precedence Daddy. Do you not realise how much you wounded me? No wonder at times my love life is fucked up, and because of my anxiety, I push men away and think, well it wasn't going to last anyway. I immediately set myself up for failure. I couldn't bear the anguish of having a relationship that lasted for years and then broke down. I wonder how Mummy coped with you walking out after 20 years, two days after winning the Eurovision song contest.

Mummy said you just came down the stairs with a suitcase not uttering a word, you put a five-pound note on the kitchen table and left. You broke her heart, and she has never got over it. She still speaks about that time, and I can see the tears well up in her eyes when she speaks about you, but she tries not to show emotion. I don't know how she carried on. In those days a divorced woman was to be frowned upon. You and Mummy's friends suddenly started shunning her, even some of your family. I remember afterwards, you told me that you were on Prozac and very unhappy. Maybe a marriage councillor would have been more appropriate than to tell than a young child, your daughter. However, I was so in awe of you at the time that whatever you said, I agreed.

You went to live with your brother and father in Stamford Hill. Two of your sisters lived in Stamford Hill and some cousins too, but I was happily staying with my Auntie Eva and Uncle Benny and my sister/ cousin Caroline and Eric in Loughton Essex. Caroline and I were the only girl cousins in the family at that time and became extremely close. I was always staying with them. They were the best times ever, and I thank my Auntie Eva for always believing in me and fighting in my corner.

Daddy if you are up there in Heaven with my lovely Auntie Eva, she will be putting you in your place, like she always did in the living world. She understood me completely. We used to go to creative writing evenings every week and in the evening's poetry readings. I remember her telling me not to read out a certain poem. Of course, I did, but she appreciated the rebel in me. Sometimes I read my poetry out in wine bars and clubs.

She was the most amazing woman. She influenced my life in such a huge way. Her Darling husband, my Uncle Benny, he would do anything for his family. The most memorable memory I have of him is when having been on a calorie-controlled diet with my cousin. I was so hungry. My cousin said I could go into the kitchen and take a slice of the cake that I was told not to touch. I did not need any persuading... In the middle of the night, I went downstairs to the larder and filled my mouth with the chocolate cake I wasn't meant to touch. Of course, it started off as a thin slice, but I kept cutting it to straighten out the edges. The Cream was oozing out of it which I smoothed out with my fingers. It tasted amazing. Thick brown chocolate and cream, I couldn't control myself.

My Uncle Benny heard a noise and thought it was burglars. Eventually, he found the disturbance, me, in the larder gorging on the chocolate cake. He asked what I was doing, he soon saw the cream and chocolate smeared all over my cheeks and mouth. It makes me laugh even today.

I loved being with them and never wanted to return to my house. All I can say is thank goodness for the times I lived with them. I had never experienced an abundance of family love as I did when I stayed with them, they were my second Mummy and Daddy, and I belonged there.

All my life I searched for that wonderful love. Thank goodness I have it at home with my children even though there was no man present, just two very short-lived marriages. When I look at my children and grandson, I am filled with pride. I got it right.

I remember speaking to someone who had also been in a coma and he told me, people that have gone through what we have, feel emotions a hundred times more. The years of fighting for your love have taken its toll. The years of rejection have affected me dreadfully. I carried around deep sadness. I was the broken girl that was sent from one place to another.

She told me in no uncertain terms that she didn't want me around. She had no reason to hate me with a vengeance, but she did, and you let her treat me like I was a piece of shit that you wipe off your shoes, you let her talk bad about me to you behind my back. Did you really agree with her? You must have.

What hold did she have on you, after all, she wasn't much to look at, in fact, she was quite plain, and when you first met her she was overweight and that, I couldn't understand, as you were so particular about weight, so what was it? Did she know things about you that you didn't want others in your showbiz life to know? Well it must have been something, but to this day I don't know.

What I do know is she was a woman who was childless out of choice. She hated kids. She never wanted to have kids, and that is probably why in later life I never got invited to family functions at your house. She would have had to have my kids, your grandchildren, there, too. She just couldn't bear that. She just wanted me out of your life, full stop. You didn't want me around either Daddy, did you? There is a large part of me that has been rejected by you, and I have had to fight for your attention.

I was cast aside like a rag doll. This rejection will stay with me forever, the same as that petrified child who has been living inside of me. Her flesh is wrapped so tightly around my internal organs and brain that we have merged into one person.

If I could look at my life objectively without some stupid loyalty to you, I would feel desperately sorry for that girl who was betrayed and tossed aside. Feelings aren't tangible, but that is not to say that they don't exist. They are like footprints in the sand, but you know they existed. I thought you were a good father in my childhood years, although you were away on business a lot, and that made it even harder to accept the change in you.

The love you shrouded me in, when I was a small little girl, was a place I wished to remain forever, in that cocoon of warmth and love. Growing up, I felt protected. Everyone in the family looked up to you, as you were the Godfather, the head of the family with your sister Eva the oldest sister (my second Mummy.)

My Aunty Eva intuitively knew how I felt. I remember her writing a poem about me and my life, which explained that even though I was living in one room, I am away from all the sadness and negativity in my life and that was spot on. I remember my Auntie reading it out to you, and you got really angry about it. You didn't want to hear the truth, did you? I so adored being at her house. It was full of love and laughter, so unlike our home, with its really awful atmosphere, I think even children can feel when their parents are not getting on. Some mornings I felt I could cut the tension in the air with a knife.

You were my hero. My big strong, successful Daddy, always working abroad or in the recording studios with your acts. You always bought back wonderful presents from overseas. I wish I still had that elegant Geisha doll that turned around to the sound of a beautiful Japanese song. Her red satin Kimono that glistened as it caught the light turning around on the large black base. The real Hermes Scarf you brought back for me and one for Mummy.

I put it in the drawer with my other clothes when I lived with you, but when I got back from living abroad, it had disappeared, along with all my other belongings. In fact, all my clothes and ornaments had been thrown out. My bedroom was replaced with a study for you and her, a room where she practised Buddhism, which housed her Gohonzon and incense burner. Even the bed had been thrown out. How on earth could you have let a woman who had just moved in do this? She had thrown out everything, every trace of me, she had the room decorated, and I was whitewashed OUT!

She never apologised to me or put them in black bin bags and stored them for me till I returned, like normal people did, No, she didn't want any traces of me left in your house, and you knew she did it, and you allowed her to do it. I remember her telling me after that she had found a lot of creams and pills of mine that she had to throw away. She then branded me, apparently a hypochondriac like you. You allowed her; you gave her the power to talk down to me. You let her rule the roost. I was never shown respect by either of you. I am sure that if I had remained married, it would have been another story, if I had a man to stand up for me. Are these the days of equality? A woman on her own is treated differently, which is why I have had to be that much more assertive.

In Hadley Common, do you remember how you used to smoke those long brown cigarettes and bring home cartons that were put high up in the tall wooden hallway cupboard? I used to take packets and smoke them in the bathroom I shared with my brother with the window open.

You know I still have recurring dreams about that house in Hadley Common. I dream that Mummy never sold it and we are all still living there as one happy family, and I feel euphoric. Spiritually I think I am still attached to that house. I tried to end my life there Daddy, the screams of a tortured soul.

I was recuperating for nearly a year after my horrific car accident that still haunts me to this day. The doctor came every day, trying to get me to write and walk and talk again. I used to walk with a limp. In just one second, my mood would change, and I would scream out at the top of my voice. I felt like I had to let this evil spirit that possessed my body go like an exorcist. Mummy told me I should let it all out. I couldn't control myself from screaming, probably delayed shock from the accident and coma I had been in.

Daddy, each day has been a struggle for me. I still can't write for a long time, or my hand is in a lot of pain... There are subtle things that I can sometimes get away with, but people have commented like eating a meal and all the food collecting at the side of my mouth—not being able to remember to sip coffee and having copious amounts in my mouth that I must swallow slowly in case of choking. I am so used to this, until people comment. I think as I have aged, these indiscretions are noticed by my nearest and dearest.

I have spent most of my life trying to get back your love. Do you know the depth of my disappointment and heartache, but you were never held accountable for it!

I don't want my children to feel this way. I have tried to be a good Mother. Maybe at times a bit overprotective. I never had the finances to buy them the latest trainers or mobiles, but I have learnt that being there for them is more important. I am a lioness over her Cubs. I would do anything or give them anything they needed. I remember the few times I had to beg you for money, sometimes to help pay my way and have enough food to put on the table, and you were always saying, "no no no" because you said you never had any money. I remember Mummy saying, "Well I will give you half if your Dad will pay half," but I couldn't ask you as you'd already told me no. Mummy would call you and get angry with you, to the point where you would give in and send Mummy a cheque. However, you would make sure you phoned me and insisted I pay you back every penny, knowing that I couldn't afford to.....

I remember once when Jade, my eldest daughter, was crying as she sat on the bed, she was so upset, as to her we were so poor, because we didn't have a computer. I comforted her and told her that if you have parents or even one parent that loves you, a roof over your head and food in your stomach, then you are rich.

Two of my children live with me, including my young grandson. The animals follow me around and fight to sleep with me. This is a real family Daddy, one you could have been part of, but instead, you preferred her and didn't include us in your life.

The only child that went through a bad patch is the one I depend on now; she has grown up so capable and strong. She was always your favourite too. Why had you not left her something, some money for her and her son?

I remember you being wheeled to the operating theatre in the Princes Grace Hospital. You took her hand and said that you will always look after her. Well you didn't, and you didn't look after any of us, and we are suffering emotionally and financially.

I don't bring up the past to her or remind her how I looked after her son for years because I know how much she had gone through, and she needed to express her feelings and just try and be a teenager again. I have always left the door open for her. I have never been judgemental like you were to me or abandoned her like you did to me. Night after night I stayed home with my children. She and her son's father are only in their twenties but are the perfect example of co-parenting. A lot of older parents could learn a lot from them because at the end of the day it is what the child needs.

Now my children are all grown up, I am at a different stage in my life, but if they need me, I am there for them. My mornings are taken up with trying to get Tyrone and my grandson awoken... Make sure all their clothes are clean and encourage them both to do study and do their homework. I like to cook for them a homemade meal as both their appetites are ferocious. Tyrone alone eats enough for a family of four. However, on the odd occasion, he will cook for me. I always made sure my children were able to cook from a young age; it is a survival skill every child should know.

Most mornings, I pray to be a better person and Mother. I never want them to feel the way you made me feel.

Your death has affected us all. The grandchildren you only saw for a couple of hours once a month or once every six weeks are grieving for you. Tyrone came back from school to tell me that he had his hour of bereavement counselling. He said he is going to make a box of memories about you.

It breaks my heart that he has gone from being in the top classes at school with Marks of 7 and 7 plus to just Marks of 2 and 3. He is such a polite and quiet boy. From the day he was born, he has never given me a moment's worry, until you passed away.

He has not only become more withdrawn, but he is not studying. He wanted to become a solicitor at one point. He has the brains for it, but your death has affected him so much. He returns from school and sleeps. He has just started socialising with his friends again after school for an hour. I am so worried about him.

Your dying has affected him so much. You were his male role model. Why, I don't know? When we went to you, for two hours, he would sit on the leather sofa quietly, and when you talked to him, he would savour every single word, with his little startled eyes behind black-framed glasses.

He would even help her take the food out on the table. I wonder what he could put in his memory box, because you never left him anything. Everything is left to her; it is like we never existed. She has completely blanked us. Don't you think as part of the grieving process your grandchildren should have been allowed to go to your flat?

I am struggling and on antidepressants, but I leave things in G-Ds hands. I focus on the things I do have. Your dying has bought up an enormous amount of pain and sorrow. I am having financial problems and having Mummy's partner driving me mad again, overstepping the boundaries, interfering again. It makes me so stressed, and I tend to overreact. I had you and her who wasn't interested in me, yet on the other hand, I have Mummy and her partner who interfere all the time. That is normal that's families for you.

I have been suffering from pharyngitis recently, which made me feel like I had the flu, so I took a cab home from the supermarket as I had come over all dizzy. It's times like these that I am thankful Mummy and her partner live close by, although he sometimes comes here too often. He is kind and mows the grass for me, but yesterday as soon as I returned home, he started banging on the door and shouting through the letter-box like he always does. I answered the door and in he barged with my daughters old Kardashian T-shirt, Denim shorts and green ankle Wellington boots. He told me I needed to see something. I could not believe my eyes. Without permission, he had butchered the ivy that was shielding me from the neighbours very high concrete extension.

I told him that he shouldn't have done it and when he left, I started crying, but actually, now I'm mentally in a better place and we all laugh about it. What I used to consider as interference, I now know is part of care and love and that's what real families do. As you Daddy never offered to ever to come to my house and help out with anything, I thought that what Max did for me was interfering as I never had a normal father/daughter relationship with you. You were always the Distant Father. Maybe If I had a man around, this would not be happening. I immediately thought that whenever things got out of hand, I would phone you my famous Daddy and you would make everything better, I would start moaning about him down the phone to you. I wanted to call you up, but of course, you are no longer here.

I am a grandmother, and I just want to live quietly now. I don't want people interfering in our life. I deserve so much more and an easier life.

In a few months' time, you would have been dead for a year, and yet I still find this grieving process unbearable, even though you left us nothing. What father does that?

Facebook shared a photo memory of you in Hyde Park today, being pushed in a wheelchair, I was there, we all had lunch in the Cafe, but it was heart-breaking that you would not eat. It was at that point it dawned on me that your days were numbered. All those years of her limiting what you ate, her diets that you had to follow, funny how now they had no importance as you were wasting away.

I love you Daddy

RIP xxx

Letter 3

Dear Daddy,

The one saving grace that usually motivates me and gives me a purpose to my day is walking round to the infamous coffee shop. Even then, I have had times where my tears mixed with the coffee. Instead of criticising my behaviour Daddy, I think you should have realised that we couldn't all be as wonderful as you or her. Well, that is what you both thought. I could list both of your flaws, but I accept that everyone has their own challenges to get through the days.

I remember when I lived with you in Westbourne Terrace Mews, you actually called out an electrician because the light bulb needed changing, or a plumber because the toilet got blocked. A testament to the fact that when it came to practical things, you were useless, but a talent when it came to writing songs and managing The Brotherhood of Man.

The coffee shop reminds me of when I used to work, etc.

There was excitement in taking the tube and being a part of the human race. The men would be on their phones or reading a newspaper while the ladies all put on their war paint ready to face the challenges of the day. There was a real buzz when I travelled to work. Frustratingly walking slowly behind someone to reach the exit and trying to overtake them was an impossibility.

It reminded me of follow the leader as we all followed each other like worker ants on the crowded platform after we had poured out of the train. Taking the stairs towards the escalator, body odour, aftershave, perfume, and the stale smell of urine mingled in the air. Standing on the right of the escalators there would always be someone in a hurry that would run down the stairs and hit you with their heavy rucksack. It made me feel alive.

Having my babies made me realise that raising them was more important. I enjoyed everything about bringing them up, but I was never really free. Those are the sacrifices a single parent makes. I never chose to be a single parent. I married twice; it wasn't my fault they were useless. I must blame my taste in men and the haphazard way I entered a marriage because I was pregnant. I never think things through, I just go with the flow.

I know I deserved so much more. Years of having to compete for your attention, Daddy, had a profound effect on me. If a man showed interest in me, because of my lack of self-worth, I would entertain him. Growing up with you as a popular, successful man in the music business, I never felt I was good enough. Whatever I did in my life was criticised, it could never compare to you.

Do you remember when you had your offices in ATV music, 25 Bruton Street and I would help you with the

Brotherhood of Man fan club? I would send signed black and white photos to fans who had requested one. I would go with you and the rest of ATV music employees and frequent a wine bar, the infamous Serafino's. It was so exciting, such a good vibe in that place. Occasionally we would go to Morton's Wine Bar in Berkeley Square.

When I went to Corona stage school, I would sometimes take my friends there, and we would have a meal and drinks. I would put everything on the tab. You told me many years later that you knew. I also knew the black cab phone number and account number off by heart. I used them so many times. I was living a privileged life. Money was abundant, and I never had to think of it, a contrast to how I am living today.

You were very successful, and I relished the time we spent together. You were Tony Hiller, the renowned songwriter and my father. Even when I was living with you in Westbourne Terrace Mews, you were hardly home, always on tour with your group, but I felt I was so lucky to be a part of your life.

I always start these letters off with *Dear Daddy* because that is what children call their Daddies or even Dad. But, you stopped being a Daddy a long time ago.

You only saw us once a month or once every six weeks as long as she could fit us in the diary, when you would perform your fatherly duties.

You would call me up and say put this in your diary. I am going to see you Sunday a week. Then I would here you shout out, Babe, Babe, is that okay? Usually, I would hear her say that you were both out at some party and you would come back with another date. It didn't matter that one of the kids had a party to go to that wasn't important to you. You used to tell me that was the only date that you could see me.

I thought this behaviour from a father was normal and acceptable. I was just happy to have some of your time. After all, you were an important successful manager and songwriter. I was just your daughter, a twice-divorced mother of three. How did that compare to your life? She was a childless woman. I don't know what she did, except to make crap food and tell you what to eat and wear. You see Daddy, I had always fought to have your time. You were a successful man; we were just your kids that a lot of people didn't even know existed, because it was always about you and her.

She owned you, and apparently, your past was erased. After all, you walked out on us when I was at my most vulnerable still recuperating from the accident. You walked out because you couldn't handle it and you didn't want to handle it as it interfered with you going on tour with The Brotherhood of Man or working in the studios and not coming home until the early hours of the morning. No wonder Mummy wasn't happy.

I grew up feeling a lot of friction between you and her. At times I felt I could cut the atmosphere with a knife. My respite was always staying around my Auntie and Uncles house with my cousins. It was a wonderful atmosphere there, and they were my second Mummy and Daddy. I had so much attention from them, and I felt truly loved.

I never had to phone up Mummy to make an appointment to see her, I would just turn up at her door and the children and I would be welcomed with open arms. We could never do that to you. I couldn't just call you and say "Dad I'm in the west end I'm popping in for a coffee and a catch up." No way, I could never do that, I was only allowed in your home by appointment..

I could never just turn up ... I just couldn't, because she didn't allow it or want it. I grew up thinking this was normal and all kids had to make an appointment to see their fathers, so I thought all fathers were like you. You never did fun things with us. You never babysat or took us away or had family trips to the seaside. It was just once a month or a six weekly lunch when you did your family duty. The lunches were always a bit strained and awkward. I used to have to give my children long pep talks beforehand the way a manager does to his football team. I told them just sit down don't run around be careful not to break anything blah blah blah and If Pappy asks just to say everything is okay.

You, of course, thought you were the best Father in the World by giving us a bit of your time, every 4 to 6 weeks, slotting us in between partying with friends or working in the studio. For G-D's sake, we were your flesh and blood. There was always tension around the table. We always had to act that everything was tickety boo. If my daughter and I exchanged words, you would shake your head in disapproval and tut at us accusing us of hating each other, which was so far from the truth. We couldn't show any emotion in front of you or her. This was hard for me, as I am an emotional, passionate woman. I wanted to have a conversation with you like we used to. There were so many things I wanted to tell you, but you asked questions to my children and never directly to me. It was though you couldn't bear to look at me or speak to me, had that wicked Bitch really got into your head so deeply that she turned you against me?

The conversation was not organic; it was stilted. The meal was always the same, bagels with smoked salmon and one plate of salad. I asked once if she would make two. I even had to bring pitta bread to go with the hummus. I remember how cringeworthy it was that you insisted we all had to applaud her for preparing us a meal. You clapped her and was always telling her over twenty times how delicious the food was, when all she made was frozen fish fingers and chips. You kept on insisting we applaud her and got quite angry with us when we were reluctant to do so.

In the end, we did because you ordered us too and you kept thanking her, you should have just got down on the floor and kissed her feet, you were pathetic. She wasn't very pleased when none of us liked her fish pie. It was simply a piece of salmon with pastry over it and no sauce. I had never seen or tasted anything like that in my life. I hope I never will again!

The fuss she would make over giving us one tiny spoonful of ice cream was rather pathetic. The minuscule portion of vanilla ice cream, never a deviation on the flavour, would accompany home-made cheesecake from an Auntie. I always make my children a homemade cooked meal in the evening like any other Mother. I don't expect a standing ovation. You cook for people, and they eat it, end of. When I look back on it, I find it so amusing.

These days, I should be in a different stage of my life now, not worrying about where the next penny is coming from. Starting on the pills again after a week's break has me worried. I can't function properly without them; I am dependant on them now. I don't like to be dependent on anything or anyone because I can't be hurt again, but at this moment in time, I need them. I love the feeling of being relaxed and able to fall asleep whenever I want. It must be like being permanently stoned. After years of taking amphetamines in the form of diet pills, I think I prefer to feel chilled.

I just live every day, not planning my future because after I nearly died just crossing the road, I do not plan anything. All I can do is pray to G-D that he will keep my family safe and healthy and provide. I don't know how you could not have provided for your grandchildren and me. It keeps cropping up in my head time and time again. It is unheard of and baffling, especially as you were a successful man.

Even Joe Blogs down the road would leave his daughter something. She may think that she has won the battle, but no one can ever take away our memories. It is obvious that you never really loved us after all. You told us numerous times that you would look after us. Your wonderful lady, as you often called her, has snubbed us. We all tried to be there for her, but she doesn't want to know. Whenever we suggest coming to see her, she tells us that she is going away. However, through other family members we find out that she is at home and not away like her text messages state.

We give up now. How many times can one extend the hand of friendship? We have tried and tried, and we are no longer going to be made fools of. I did tell you about her snide comments to me over the years which you just brushed away. Her telling me not to call you, but you were always in awe of her, and you always obeyed. You saw everything in rose-tinted spectacles. Daddy, I get that you deserved to have love in your life from a partner as we all do, but did it mean you had to distance yourself from my children and me.

I think over the years, of her pushing me out of your life, you forgot about our closeness and friendship, but if I dig deep into my memory Daddy, I ask you now, was we ever really that close? It pains me that I don't really have many memories of my young childhood years. It's like most things that happened before my accident have been erased from my memory, and all I remember is what happened after. She wanted you to forget about your past. However, how can you forget your own daughter? How can you moan to everyone about me? When I was once your little Princess and you smothered me with love. We can forget a lot of things but not pushing your own daughter aside for someone else. It is something I will never forget or forgive.

I almost forgot about the group you entered in The Eurovision, years after The Brotherhood of Man. I remember so clearly you are handing me a huge wad of cash and telling me I had great fashion sense. Could I go and choose four outfits for the group—two for the men and two for the women. I went to St. Christopher's Place and on the corner was a boutique. I picked out gold leather outfits, all a variation of each other. You were really pleased with my choice. I introduced you to a band you worked with because I had heard them sing in a club and thought they were really good. That was all before she brainwashed you.

That was when you did think my opinion and knowledge counted for something...

We went to so many showbiz parties together with Eric Hall, in fact, you two were always together, but like me, she didn't want him coming around to the flat. You had walked out of my life once before when I was vulnerable and young, recovering from the Trauma of the accident, mentally and physically. I had to do dramatic things to gain your attention, and this was to happen again, once you met her.

I must question whether I was crazy as you told everyone. Did you really think I was crazy, Daddy? If you tell someone time and time again the same thing, they tend to believe it. The human body is wonderful, it can repair itself, but when someone has such a harrowing experience as I did, the mind will never forget. All one can do is try to live the best way I can. Can you believe Daddy I am suffering from PTSD? Apparently, the traumatic experience from my accident is lodged at the front of the brain and should be at the back, which is why I am still having flashbacks of that period when I was in hell.

I say hell because that is the only word to describe it. Lying on a bed in a semi-conscious state but not being able to move any part of my body. I was paralysed, and that is what has affected me most. I recall that time with such fear and horror. I never ever want that to happen to me again. When I think about it, the tears start to form and slide down my face. I am transported back to that time; I remember lying paralysed on the bed completely locked in my body. Is it any wonder I went on to develop claustrophobia? I particularly remember lying helpless on the hospital bed many times, staring into the darkness and telling myself that this is just a very bad dream. If I shut and open my eyes again, this will be a bad dream, but that bad dream went on and on, spilling into my future. I used to fear falling asleep in case I returned to that time. I couldn't tell you how I felt or what I was going through, as you and she spoke in such a condescending way to me, like I was an idiot and you were both intellects, and you both believed you were right about everything. In fact, it took me over 20 years to be able to talk about it.

So, there I was sat in the coffee shop engrossed in my phone, my brother came up and said hello. He doesn't come around to the house; he hasn't bothered to see his nieces or nephews. In fact, he is a terrible Uncle, but you and Mummy allowed him to behave like that. He seemed to be the golden boy. I got the blame for everything. If I had died in the car accident, you would never have had grand and great-grandchildren, but I don't think that would have bothered you as your brothers and sisters and your music career was more important to you.

Your show business persona of yours was how I judged you a father. I put you on a pedestal. However, Tony Hiller the successful Songwriter, Producer, and Publisher obliterated the real facts, if fathers were measured by their parenting skills you would have been bottom of the list, Daddy. After I found out what you told Amber, my daughter, I was disgusted with you, do you remember what you told her Daddy? "I only bothered with your Mother cos I felt sorry for her after the accident" What kind of father says that? How dare you after what I went through and after what I'm still going through?

My brother and I exchanged pleasantries until I could not hold it in anymore. " you and your wife see her," I said knowingly, "Well please tell her that I still don't have any of Dads gold discs, or in fact anything to remember him by, He was after all our father, and whether she likes it or not, he did have a family before he met her"

He asked how many I wanted. I did not think I had to ask for a specific number, but I asked for 5—one for each of my children and one for my grandson.

I explained to him that each of us is grieving. His nephew, he doesn't bother with, like all his nieces and his nephew who is having bereavement counselling.

He should have more compassion for them as they are his flesh and blood. He should be helping us, but like most people, they are under her spell just like you were Daddy.

I also asked for one of your Ivor Novelo awards which Keith immediately replied was not possible as she helped him get them? What? She helped you get them for songs that you wrote before you even met her, did she now claim to have co-written songs with you, the ones you had written before she came into your life? To be honest, I was rather overcome with emotion and told my brother to send her a message which I am sure he told her as soon as he got home, which put a smile on my face. You see I don't care anymore, Daddy. If I have something to say I will say it and I don't need your approval.

I love you Daddy

RIP xxx

Letter 4

Dear Daddy,

As in life, so it was in death. I wasn't able to be a part of your funeral. She told me that she had asked my brother to help her organise everything. There was a problem with obtaining the death certificate due to a Bank Holiday. The family wanted you to be cremated as soon as possible, but it was not to be. As you stated in your will you wanted to be cremated. To think of you in a freezer for days was upsetting.

The whole cremation had been arranged by a cousin's wife and my brother. They had taken over the whole thing. Imagine how I felt, learning when my father's cremation was going to be on someone's Facebook page. My daughters and I had offered to visit her and comfort her, but she always had an excuse. The usual one being that she was going away. I would think that a loving woman who had lost her husband would want to be with the daughter and grandchildren of the man she had loved. But we are talking about a manipulative, cold, calculating woman. We know as decent people that we had done the right thing by you. She never liked us when you were living, so why should she change now? In fact, her true colours had come out. My texts to her were sometimes unanswered. As per usual, I felt invisible.

I had to find out when my own father's funeral was from Facebook. You always told me you detested Facebook, however just recently I found out that you did in fact have not only a Facebook page but an Instagram account too. Why did you tell me you never had any social media Daddy? Was it because you didn't want me as a friend on your social media or did someone else decide that for you?

Your home address was all over Facebook and your granddaughter Amber didn't think it right because she was living alone. We mentioned this only out of concern, but as usual, we were victimised. We were only trying to protect her, posting your personal address on Facebook, really? The whole week running up to the funeral, I was aware of wicked, hurtful remarks about Amber and me. The texts were sent to another cousin. Apparently, a security guard was being hired, and if need be, we would be thrown out of your flat. In fact, you did say it was my brothers and my flat, but she could live in it till she died? I really don't understand that Daddy, not when she has two other properties, in total the three properties are worth millions. Do you know how hard my life has been and still is? I can't work at the moment, and I have the responsibility still of two of your grandchildren and my grandson living with me.

I don't understand why she never liked us and why you were scared to voice your opinion? She told you how to live your life, whom you could be friends with, whom you were allowed to work with, what to eat and how to dress. She probably, in my opinion, told you to write another will when you had the onset of dementia. I knew you had written a will a very long time ago, but this was to be surprisingly changed! You promised that you would always look after me financially and yet you left everything to her?

Daddy, you know how I am struggling, I can't work with people, my anxiety and depression won't let me and every day I have to cope with my depression and crazy thoughts. I am not a team player in many respects.

The children were so upset at losing their Pappy. Tyrone, your grandson, is now having counselling. Of course, all the cousins rallied around the grieving widow. Did I ever count? But the children and I had each other. No one has ever called to ask how the children and I are, but Im not surprised really as none of you and her friends even knew we existed.

She had primarily chosen my brother to get the death certificate and arrange your Shiva. How hypocritical when you never believed in God or religion. The so-called family wanted to make it Jewish.

Note: A Shiva in the Jewish religion is when the Rabbi comes and says prayers for the deceased's close family in the evening. The close members of the family must sit on low chairs separate from the visitors. The idea of sitting on low chairs is to feel humble and connected to the earth below. Men aren't allowed to socialise and work. They cannot shave either, the same as women who are not meant to apply makeup hence the reason why mirrors are covered up. Shiva is the Hebrew word for seven which is the number of days people mourn for.

Apparently Daddy you only wanted a Shiva for one day. In your flat, in the lounge, as you know, the whole of one wall is mirrors, so it was impossible to cover them up.

I don't think the funeral arrangements were going smoothly. To not even be asked to help showed her hate and utter disrespect towards me. She always socialised with my brother and his wife. Well, she would, wouldn't she, they never had kids, some medical reason from both of them, so they were welcomed. I bet if they had kids like me, they wouldn't have been welcome neither. This was a regular occurrence over the years. I wasn't invited to family parties. I was completely excluded. On the odd occasion, I was at a family function, you and she would make your entrance, and I always went up to you, to be respectful to her and you would give me a kiss and ask if I was alright? She would just fake a smile like a Cheshire cat, don't you think that hurt me? You never stood with me. She didn't want us to be close.

You know Daddy the more I recount things, the more I realise how unfairly I had been treated by you both. She must have put a spell on you; it was as if you hated me. You were always very tactile with her and calling her Mummy. Once when cousin Eric was talking to you and you never put down the receiver on the phone properly. He overheard the whole conversation even down to when she told you what a naughty boy you had been. You had to stand in the corner facing the wall. You and Eric were family, firm friends and business associates. She made sure he didn't come around to the house anymore. She used to control everything you ate down to the exercise you took. It was just as well you ate out most of the time as her idea of a portion was minuscule not something familiar to a Jewish man whose mother was a sensational cook.

When you and Eric had a large lunch together, you would go to the shop after and buy your favourite Yorkie chocolate bars. You would beg Eric not to tell her and seemed genuinely worried. I wonder what she would have done to you. I know for a fact she used to call you a naughty boy. Maybe that was how your relationship was.

What made you get cremated? It is something that is not usually the thing to do if one is Jewish. You never believed in G-D or religion, did you? Your body was left in a freezer for days. Eric, my cousin, said that you deserved a big showbiz send off and a few more days wouldn't make any difference. It would give your music business friends around the world the time to arrange travel and accommodation, but it had to be done quickly to fit around one of your brothers, who was only here for a few days from America.

Since you have been gone Daddy, I haven't been able to cope with this grieving process, but it has been so much more than that, The Dr said it had exasperated my other issues. I cut my arm and let the blood drip, so my physical pain would show the devastation and heartache I was feeling inside. You were my sticky plaster that covered the cuts and grazes, or so I thought.

In hindsight, it was all in my mind, you were never truly the doting proud father I had created in my mind. You were the one I called up to get advice on a situation as I wasn't able to vent how I felt to you in person, as you would quieten me up. Sssssssh Sssssssh you would shut your eyes and almost spit out the last Sssssssh, your hand up at your face and fists clenched. I only had to listen to you.

You had this way of cutting me short, not listening, only listening to the sound of your own voice because you were God. You knew everything. You dismissed my intelligence and had this way of keeping me down. You told everyone in the family I was mad. I was mad and I bled you dry. That wasn't true Daddy. You wouldn't even buy my house cheaply with Mummy when it was offered, and you had the millions to do it at that time.

What about the time I cried down the phone begging you for a car to drive my kids and grandson to schools to the shops and days out for the kids, I didn't ask for a brand new expensive car just a second-hand cheap car, I would have been so grateful for that. I told you I was having physiotherapy because I had pulled all my muscles carrying heavy bags of shopping. You promised to buy me a car as a gift, I couldn't believe it at the time, but actually, it was a cheap second-hand car that kept breaking down and cost more to repair than what it was worth. I couldn't afford to get it fixed so it was left parked outside the house, but I was still paying you back for a car I couldn't use.

In your kitchen stands a huge fridge that makes ice and you could drink ice-cold water directly from it, but when my little fridge jammed packed with food broke down, for the cost of one of your meals in a restaurant you refused to go half with Mummy to buy me another one, I only asked you for a second-hand fridge, 50 quid that's all it was second hand, I only asked you for 25 quid as Mummy was going to pay the other half, God forbid I should ask you for something new. Everything I had was second hand or hand me downs.

You told me I should do what she does and order food online. Daddy, first of all, I didn't have a computer, I couldn't afford one, but you didn't know as you didn't care, you didn't really know the woman I am, I like to feel and see what I buy. I like the local shops that sell quality food, and I prefer my meat to be halal because I do not like the after taste of blood. This is me, Daddy, you never embraced my individuality you just wanted me to live the way you wanted, but I am my own unique person. I am proud of who I am and what I have done.

I want to know why you built her up to be a Goddess when all the men I chose were never good enough for you. You would always make fun of my choices and me. Why did you make me feel like a complete failure? You need not have worried as in true form my relationships like my two marriages finished quickly, after all, Daddy, none of them could compare to you.

I remember when I was just 15, I had met a young man at the Wimpy Bar in Stamford Hill. You didn't like him either. At that particular time, I was at my secondary school and was being bullied for living in a large house in Hadley Wood. I remember how it started: a boy called Anthony was sitting on the desk, not at it but on the edge at the front of those wooden desks where there was a hole to put ink in for your fountain pen, not that this class bothered with fountain pens but my previous convent school did. He peered over noisily at the registrar and came across my name and address. "You live in that big house, don't ya'?" His eyes looked into mine and I remember how I felt to this day. 'Watcha doing, going to this school?' All eyes were on me. I just wanted to blend in with everyone as I always do and still do. Especially after the car accident and having to leave school because of all the cruel bullying I had to endure.

Ever since your stroke you had started deteriorating, shuffles now replaced your walks. You always forgot your great-grandson's name preferring to call him Howie, his name is Harvey. You thought one of my daughters was me. Is that why you became the way you did? I remember when the kids and I came to see you, this was on your 91st birthday. You kept talking about it for ages, that this was your goal, to keep alive forever. You were scared of Death.

In the end she got her claws into you and you treated me like I was a nuisance and not your only daughter. I loved you so much, Daddy, I would listen to you and take your advice because you were God in my eyes.

Do you remember her suggestion that instead of going to your flat anymore we would all meet up at the Iranian Restaurant in Edgware Road? We liked it there. Especially in the summer months when we ate outside in their garden. You would have to bring your own bottle of wine to the restaurant, but it was strictly prohibited for her as she was a recovering alcoholic with Hepatitis.

You met her at a Health Farm as she was a very close friend of one of your male friends. I remember meeting him and his wife a few times as we were invited to their house. He owned a factory that made underwear and I remember him giving me knickers in red and black for every day of the week, just one of the items he made. None of us is perfect and to beat an addiction is the hardest thing one can do. After all, wasn't I hooked on slimming pills? I remember going out with you on many occasions to restaurants, and you would have to taste all her desserts to see if there was any alcohol in them. This went on for years.

You also told me that she would fall asleep on the street and not know where she was in the mornings when she woke up. You used to speak about this like it was a wonderful thing but considering you always disapproved of my husbands and spoke ill of them; it is surprising who you picked. A bit hypocritical really, but then nobody dares criticise you.

The way you always sang her praises was pathetic. I never did find out her talents. Since she met you, she had never done a day's work, but was very prolific at being rude to me. I remember turning up at your flat with the children once, and she said I looked like Miss Piggy. She just put up with me for the duration of the visit. I tried so hard to be nice to her, but the truth was, she didn't want the children in her and your life and me. The way she ignored all my children is heart-breaking and just shows what a horrible human she is. Everything I did, you told me she could do better, but besides brainwashing you against the children and me she did not have any great talents.

Oh yes, I remember, she made curtains. When my oldest daughter had transitioned from being a baby to a toddler, I kept asking you if she could make me some curtains for her room. I kept asking you, months down the line on the phone, you told me she did not want to make curtains for my daughter who was your granddaughter. I asked why, and you just replied that she does not want to and that was the end of it, and I was not to ask again, after all the great Tony Hiller had spoken. I mustn't ask anything and be a nuisance.

There are a lot of things we don't want to do, but when it comes to you or your partner's family, you put your selfishness aside.

Daddy it didn't have to be like this, we could all have been a big happy family, but then you must take the blame as well. I loved you Tony Hiller, the successful songwriter and I loved you Daddy until you met her. Then I lost you, and it ripped my heart in two. I became a nuisance to you and spent 40 years trying to get back my reputation and your love. I wish I would have spoken out more. Life goes by, and we let people treat us badly because we dont want or like confrontations. I also had no self-confidence. You couldn't argue with the great Tony Hiller especially if you were his daughter.

You stopped inviting me out and pushed me as far in the shadows as possible. Don't you think it would have been nice to help me out with the children taken them out for the day or have some sleepovers? If I made a comment about something, you used to quiz me like you were a detective. You would even ask for names of people who agreed with me, insinuating that you wanted to quiz them, too. Actually, Daddy, I found it amusing, but if she told you the sky was pink with purple spots, you would believe her.

I hope you are happy up there if Heaven exists, having parties with the angels and your family and showbiz friends. I also hope your family has set you straight about the way you treated me.

Many times, as a young child with my brother on a Sunday, you would drive to Ashken's delicatessen to buy us Bagels with cream cheese and smoked salmon. I remember tearing the salmon off the skin with my teeth as my hands became oily. I would suck on the shiny skin and chew it. You also bought Tubs of egg and onion and chopped liver to go with the Platzels. You always talked of your Mother with such love, I wish I had known her.

From the deli we would go in the car you would drive to where you grew up. You were so proud of your roots—a successful man from Jewish immigrant parents. Because of Hitler, your parents fled from Poland, finding a haven in England. You told me how you and your brother Irving had to fight Mosley and the black shirts. You were my Superhero, as you told me how a mob of you used to go to the fascist meetings and knock the bastards out. I know you must have hurt them, as over the years from you and others, I heard how you should have been a professional boxer. You were a boxer at the fairgrounds too and you would box for money, with people from the crowds, but they never beat you.

Remember when I lived with you in Westbourne Terrace Mews? (Before Her) I used to pass the bathroom, and with the door ajar I would see you shadow boxing in the mirror. My strong Daddy. A real tough East End man. We had such a wonderful time, although you were often away touring with the Brotherhood of Man. One of the first things she couldn't wait to tell me and to hurt me even more, was that you told her, when I lived with you, they were the worst days of your life. Did you really say that?

I love you Daddy

RIP xxx

Letter 5

Dear Daddy,

You never left anything to me, not even a watch to remember you by. I wonder if the chain with a razor blade inscribed 'to Our Bubala' was amongst the jewellery given to my brother. Martin Lee and Sandra Steven's of the Brotherhood of Man gave you that as a present, I remember you showing it to me. It was the punk era. The sounds of 'X-ray Specs', 'Johnny Rotten', and 'Sham 69'. I should know, the times I danced to music. I remember hitting my head on the spiral staircase, getting a black cab to various venues to see a punk band play. Of course I had to make them stop two streets away, as I didn't want anyone to see me get out of a Taxi, as that is not what real punk rockers did. I remember having a job down Petticoat Lane in a shop that sold Punk clothes. Those were the days.

Daddy, you were married for twenty years to Mummy, I always wanted to know, why did you walk out then? Instead of telling me lies as a child that Mummy was mad and you took Valium because of her, you should have sought professional help. Are you aware that you broke three people's hearts?

When you died, I realised you were not the man I thought you were. That night after the awful time I had at the funeral, I went back with my cousin/sister to stay with her at her friend's house. She made me realise how much I had hurt Mummy and given her such a hard time, because of you Daddy. You made her my enemy, brainwashing me against her from a child, telling me and others that she was Mad and Bad. Exactly what you said about me to everyone.

I fell apart and sobbed my heart out and felt a strong urge to phone my Mummy and tell her I was so sorry for all the times I had hurt her based on what you had told me. At least Mummy and I are building bridges now. Thank God I am able to make amends while she is still alive, or I would never have forgiven myself for the rest of my life.

I thought you were so cool, Daddy, never interfering in my life. Still, the truth is you never interfered because you had no interest in me and obviously couldn't care less about my little family and me. On the other hand, Mummy would drive me mad, phoning every day or sending her partner around to my house to see if we were all okay. I know now that's because Mummy loved and cared about my wellbeing and her grandchildren.

Grieving is a subject that is never discussed enough in Western Worlds. Maybe that is why people feel the need to accumulate great amounts of cash and material things. Somehow people think they can barricade themselves and surround themselves with material things, but those material things don't get transported to the other side. We can't take them with us when we die. The most important thing is family. The love you left behind and a lifetime of memories.

Most parents who have wealth, usually leave something to better their children's life but not you. Coming from such a large family as yours, I would have thought you had the blueprint to be more involved with me. You and Mummy had been so good at wrapping me in cotton wool and dictating how I should live my life when I was younger. I know that if I had married a good strong man, then my life would have been so different. Maybe I should have concentrated on that. As much as I wanted it, I also wanted to be free. The shackles of the past determined my future. Part of me died when I had the accident. Somehow, your dying has relieved a lot of pain and heartache.

It was me who insisted a memorial plaque should be put upon the wall in Golders Green Crematorium to honour your life, but my children and I have yet to see it, maybe we will, one of these days. You weren't an ordinary person; you were a successful songwriter / record producer.

Your plaque is on the wall with other great singers, producers' songwriters etc. One of your most famous songs, 'United we Stand' was used for the 9/11 Memorial Day. I was really so proud of you. It was also used as the song in the advert for United Airlines.

They are selling Father's Day cards in the shops which are obsolete to me. When I think of the dramatic things I had to do to get your attention, it breaks my heart.

I always said the wrong things, or got too emotional, I got tongue-tied when I was with you face to face, but as I could only talk to you once every 4 weeks and even then, I had to try and catch your attention in between the children. Everything that I wanted to tell you which had built up inside of me for weeks just came blurting out of my mouth all jumbled up.

Let's be brutally honest. Money is power, and money buys your freedom. Today I went to the bank, but no money had come into my account. I got home and started crying. Some days it all gets too much, and I just want to run away. Do you think that if I had money I would be living here? Mummy and her partner are a few doors away, and I have to go home the long way sometimes in case they see me walking past the house. She lends me money, and if I can't pay her back, she goes on and on. I feel like a little girl because her man friend of over 30 odd years thinks he has the right to speak rubbish to me and yet Mummy is the one with the purse strings. I avoid them as I can't take the stress, but deep down, what would I prefer? A parent that couldn't give a damn about me or one that admittedly gets a bit overpowering but who loves and cares about me?

I sometimes think I would be better off in eternal sleep, but whilst one is living, there is always hope. Hope that someone will wave a magic wand, and that person should have been you, you were the one who could and should have done it! You told us how much you loved us and that you would always take care of us. Words are cheap, but the truth is you never. You were so successful when I was a small child. I felt I was so loved by you. I grew up believing that it did not matter what I did as my Daddy was very successful and would always take care of me. How wrong could I have been? I never thought about you meeting another woman, especially a woman that was completely ignorant to family values. I was very pleased for you, but instead of us all being a family unit, she did everything possible to split us up.

Obviously, you couldn't have loved us, but I tend to think something not absolutely legal went on. Unless I had hundreds and thousands of pounds to go to court with, no one will ever know. Money is freedom, and I want to find my wings. I have been trapped in this life for too long.

God gave me the talent to write and more recently paint, but not a business brain to promote my work. I have had a few successes and been in the media. Writing to you each day is making me feel stronger.

Now that Tyrone will be turning 17 this year and the girls are women, I think I deserve to spread my wings and be free. I am a good woman and deserve someone to love and look after me. Why should I be in this position now? You have always done what you wanted, and now that I am at this stage in my life, I want to be that woman sitting with her partner on a Sunday afternoon, going for long walks, and reading the newspaper with him. I want to be driving the car to the supermarket and not walking back with heavy bags of shopping or having to worry about how I will pay the next bill. I have no one to tell me that I have to stay at home and be with the children, but I have no one to travel with and experience different cultures. I am pleased to say that I beat my phobia a few months after you died.

Maybe she felt threatened when she saw the things I was writing on Facebook, but I was in such a bad way, you had only just died I was distraught. She contacted me then. It was the only time she had contacted me since you died and she hasn't contacted me since, so she offered me a deal, a measly amount of money compared to what she's worth now, to silence me on Facebook.

I took it, Daddy, as I had so much debt, I finally put 100 pounds deposit on a second-hand car, it was only 500 pounds, but I thought it would be nice to finally be able to go to Asda and drive my 8 bags of shopping home rather than having to walk the long trek home carrying those heavy bags. I treated my children and my grandson as I had never been able to afford to do that before, and I treated myself to a Holiday, I went to Spain and stayed with one of my cousins. That didn't cost a lot as I bought a cheap return ticket, however, it was a very much needed break for me. After all, I had not had a holiday since I was a teenager, and that holiday was paid for by my Aunt and Uncle, who took me to Spain with them. I was having a really hard time, Daddy and returning to Spain to see my cousins was my therapy.

The children and I were made to feel like strangers in your flat. I can't get this out of my mind. I will never forget this. It is your sister's 94th birthday. Your Family were all going to be there, but once again I was not invited, so once again I was excluded because she was going, and she didn't want me there.

Did you know Daddy I hadn't taken my pills for three days and because I took one again it has messed me up, I felt like my head was spinning, dizzy and sleepy, I really need to go back to the Doctor, but what's he going to prescribe? There are no pills for emotions or money problems.

You could have made our lives so much easier. For years I see women just like her, driving around in

Mercedes Jeeps and are so pampered by their partners. I don't think you realise how hard life has been for me. Sadly, I admit my taste in men was bloody awful, and my two husbands useless. I don't even get child support, but I raised them all to be decent members of society, and I am so proud of them all. Maybe I should have been more like her, married for money, but no, that's not me. I remember at your will reading, do you know what she said Daddy? You must have heard her from up there? "I've had to wait years for this." What a Bitch!!!

You never made provisions for me or the children. You dangled a carrot in front of my face and said you are leaving the flat to my brother and me, but she a childless woman with two other properties in W2 can live in the flat until she dies. She can also sell it if she wants to, she can also do whatever she wants with your investments and money that's in your Trust Fund, as she's also a Trustee of your trust fund along with your nephew, who is also her lawyer, I wonder what plans they have for all of your wealth? I thought you could have made my life easier by giving me the property now my brother and I could have sold it and we both would have been set up. I wouldn't have to continue to live on 100 pounds a week. Feed all my children and grandson, who lives with me and pay all the utility bills, what use is it in 10 or 20 years? She is younger than you. Why does she deserve to have everything? You really didn't care about us, did you? or were you not aware of what you were doing? When you made the new will?

You couldn't have loved us. Why did you not leave us anything? Everything was left to her. My Solicitor friend was in England yesterday, and I met up with him. You know, my gentleman friend that you wouldn't invite over to your house. Again, the sheer disrespect and disregard for me. Maybe you knew that he wasn't a fool because he was a Lawyer and educated.

We went over your extremely short will. You have given her everything—nothing for us. You know I don't have any money. Shame on you! How I wasted my life trying to get love back from you. The love you absolutely showered on me when I was younger. You were swinging me around the room in Chiswick. I remember on Holidays in Bournemouth I used to walk up the zig-zag path to the beach and you would put your hand on my back and gently push me up the hill. Spending your whole holiday at travel agents to make sure I had a place to stay in Israel when I was a teenager—going to all the showbusiness parties with you. Spending time with you in your offices in ATV Music, 25, Bruton Street. That address is forever etched in my mind.

Spending hours after work in Serafino's Wine bar with most of the office staff. I remember eating there with friends from stage school and signing the bill, Eating and drinking in Morten's wine bar. Such wonderful happy times which will forever be in my mind, as will all the bad times which started that day, the day she got her claws into you.

Love you, Daddy

RIP xxx

Letter 6

Dear Daddy,

I hope you knew that when you lay on your death bed, I came to see you every day. It was the only time I was allowed to see you more than once a month. Do you know how heartbreaking that was for me? Even then, I had to tell her what time I was coming and be fitted in around your showbiz friends and her personal friends. The irony of it was, time was not on your side.

The last time I saw you, I am so glad I was able to tell you that I will never forgive you for only seeing me, your daughter and my children once a month or sometimes once every six weeks and how it deeply upset me, you can never know how that made me feel.

You never told me how well I was bringing up your grandchildren; you only commented on the negative.

Did it ever occur to you, Daddy? Well, why would it? It wasn't like we were at the forefront of your mind. It has been so emotionally draining bringing up all the children as a single parent. Wondering if all the decisions I made alone were the right ones, and the hardest thing was feeling so terribly alone. I longed for someone to wipe away my tears and to put their arms around me at the end of the evening. There has been no one! Instead, I am left alone with my thoughts and anxiety to keep me company and this vast, expanse of bloody loneliness that I feel every single night.

Did you really think that I wanted this life? That I chose to be a single parent (twice divorced) and feel inadequate when everyone else was part of a couple.?

Often you would randomly comment that I had a great life. Really Daddy? You had no idea. I have been held prisoner by the choices I made, but I have honoured my responsibilities. Since I have had children, I can't seem to pull myself out of this hole as circumstances keep pulling me back.

I so want to break free and be able to choose living the rest of my life the way I want to just like you lived your life. It was so easy for you to leave your life behind and start a new one without any conscience for your casualties because you put yourself first.

I felt totally rejected, but I should have been used to it by now. Time is the most precious gift you can give someone, and obviously, we weren't worth your time. You were definitely not the doting grandfather you should have been. You never once gave me credit for bringing my children up alone, never once had you acknowledged how well I raised your grandkids. You only commented on the negative.

When one of my daughters and I spoke, you accused us of arguing we would look at each other in bemusement because we were used to your ridiculous comments. I was absolutely shocked when after expressing one day how tired I was, just in passing, you and she suggested if he's too much, I should give up my grandson for adoption. How dare you, Daddy! How dare she! He is my flesh and blood, your flesh and blood, your great-grandson. How that wicked thought could have crossed both of your minds was unthinkable. I was disgusted with the both of you for suggesting such a thing. I was shocked to the core. I only wanted to talk to you about the trials and tribulations of motherhood and grandma hood, but really I shouldn't have done that, as you were never a doting father or grandparent and she, well, she never liked or wanted children, What response did I really expect from two selfish people?

You both had a way of becoming judge and Jury in my life, telling me what I should do when none of you had a damned clue. You could just about take a few hours of your great-grandson being there. Whenever we were due to visit you whatever was going on, we agreed we would just say everything is fine, but we were all on tenterhooks, it was always the same every time we were allowed in your home, an atmosphere you could cut with a knife.

On a few occasions the only money I had left went on the train fare to go to see you but I never said anything, or you would start moaning, and I didn't need you to tell me as you always did on numerous occasions, how wonderful my life was. You had no idea, how at times I struggled. Thirty-one years later and I am still waiting for you both to have my first-born stay over at your house as you promised. To be honest none of you played the role of a grandparent You were always out with your friends attending some social event

Mummy and her partner Max always did their grand-parent duties. I never needed an appointment to see them, and if I needed them to help out with the kids, they always obliged even taking them on days out and holidays.

You both spent so many holidays abroad, but heaven forbid you would invite a grandchild with or invite us along. That was unheard of. You used to holiday abroad frequently but whenever I suggested it would be nice for me to go away with the kids you told me we never needed a holiday. We weren't entitled to one. That was so cruel. You could have paid for us to even go to the seaside. Your argument was that you never had a holiday when you were young. You were always comparing your life in the twenties and thirties to our life today. You used to speak about your mother's parenting skills—the way she took the broom to whack one of you. If I were to do that nowadays, the social services would become involved, and I would probably get arrested for child cruelty.

I am so glad I was finally able to tell you on your death bed, how I felt, what daughter has to make an appointment to see their father? Of course, for the first time ever, you couldn't answer me, you were laying dying. It is sad, tragic, and abnormal, but that is how it was. If the kids were off school, I used to tell you, hoping that you would suggest seeing your grandchildren, but you were always busy. We could only see you when you and she decided 'let me look at my book" you would say as if making an appointment to see a business client. You always had to ask her permission when you made a window for us.

We all knew it was because of her. You and she lived in a bubble. She made sure I wasn't around to burst the bubble. Remember when I went to stay in Israel when I was a teenager, how she quickly moved in with you and you stood by and let her get rid of my bedroom! You didn't even have the decency to consult me. All my things had been thrown away along with my clothes. There was not a trace of me in your 'new study and home. Did you both hope I wasn't ever going to return to the UK?

Even when you were at death's door, we were made to feel unwelcome. Did it matter when I was coming to see you, or if I was bringing any of your Grandchildren? Was it inconvenient because her friends were there? We were your flesh and blood, and you were dying; it was okay for your neighbours to come with random friends, but not us.

When you were literally hours away from passing over from life to death, the bedroom was so quiet, only the sound of your breathing was heard. For the first time, we were alone, apart from the Carer, it was an improvement to when I was fitted in to see you with other people.

Standing at the bottom of your bed while people from showbusiness were talking to you I was just there being fitted in, the little girl, whom you told, that you wrote two songs for, was that really true Daddy? The little girl that became a nuisance because you were living another life.

The very last time I came to visit you, she opened the door and immediately asked me like she was asking her cleaner in that emotionless way, if I would like a cup of tea? Yet I hadn't been able to drink a cup of tea since my second child was born, I only drink coffee, but she knew that, and that was twenty-four years ago.

I went into your bedroom. The carer was there sitting next to you. You lay motionless in the double hospital bed. A thin sheet and blanket covered your thin body, only the movement at the side of your neck moved every time you took a breath; I went up to you and stroked your forehead. You were burning hot. You were holding on because I knew like me you had a fear of dying. I looked at the open window, which was there for your soul to go through. I rather liked this imagery.

"Daddy please," I spoke softly aware that the bedroom door was open. I really wanted to close that door, so it would just be you and I, as it was when I was a young child-the wonderful Daddy that you took such an interest in me. The daddy who used to carry me on his strong, wide shoulders. The Daddy that warmed my white woollen cardigan on the heater and burnt it. I always remember the time Mummy went to the hairdressers and asked you to prepare the sausages. You put the sausages in a roasting tin and began rolling them.

You were neither inexistent nor non-existent, "you cannot stay like this Daddy. I love you so much, please go."In my mind's eye I saw your whole deceased family urging you to pass over. Many times, when you lay sedated on your death bed, I was told you shouted out your brother Irving's name. You and he were so close. You used to be a double act, The Hiller Brothers.

I told you Irving wants to come and hold your hand as you pass over to the other side. Did he come for you Daddy as your bond with him was so strong? I would love to know if you had been reunited with your deceased family. I hope so. You told me how much you missed him when he died.

I never ever thought I would see this day when my strong daddy was slipping away. Your breath smelt of death and I noticed your teeth had turned black. As I observed you from the bottom of your bed, I saw that your face was leaning to one side of your shoulder, there was a paper napkin on your right shoulder, and a brown checked tea cloth on the other. I noticed how your mouth dropped, which I had never seen before. I came and sat in the chair next to you. I could hear the rain beating against the window. I was happy to see that the small window at the top was ajar, she had listened to my request.

I googled Hebrew prayers for the dying and read them out quietly, occasionally glancing over to you.

I just wanted to be alone with you, but I was denied that privilege because you disregarded me from the moment you met her. The lady from Marie Curie walked in. I just wanted for once in years to be with you. I told her I was saying prayers for you and she left.

I read the prayers repeatedly. You weren't a religious man; in fact, whenever I mentioned God, you would tell me you never believed in him or religion. I remember visiting you as I did on many occasions in the Princess Grace hospital opposite Madame Tussauds in Baker Street.

Every week it seemed your stents which were keeping you alive got blocked. She said, without the stents, you would die. But the constant intrusive ops to mend the stents were killing you, and it was obvious the ops and procedures weren't successful. You caught superbugs in the hospital too. My daughters and I were not happy you had procedures nearly every week. Each one had an adverse effect and made you worse. Of course, our opinion was dismissed, but at what point do you halt procedures and think logically that nothing is going to work?

I remember sitting on your huge leather sofa overlooking the tiny paved courtyard that was filled with large pots of plants. You told me as you did every time you returned from the hospital, that you had experienced a horrible time, but you were going to get fitter and start walking around Hyde Park again. That was never going to happen again. I felt so sad for you Daddy because you had such mental determination; however the physical demands on a terminally ill body were incompatible. I got up from the chair after reading the Hebrew prayers for over an hour. In a way they gave me strength. I walked over to your bed and kissed your forehead; I never knew this was going to be the very last time I would see you.

I love you Daddy

RIP xxx

Letter 7

Dear Daddy,

You always seemed to favour my second daughter above all of my other children, even me. I think it was because you felt sorry for her that she had her child young. Of course, she told me that it was my fault my daughter got pregnant. I should have put her on the pill or made her have an abortion. Well, I was the Mother, and I feel that every child is a blessing from God. I was not going to force her to have a termination like you forced me! Your mother had her first child around that age. I cannot imagine life without my grandson. The happiness he brings us all is magical. That is what life is all about.

I am struggling financially, Daddy, but I am rich with having close wonderful children. We have such a close bond. Considering you and your siblings were very close, I am amazed that you were such a terrible example of a grandfather and a bad father. I am called by my grandson "My Nanny" Like my son he always tells me he loves me. I remember you told everyone you felt sorry for me because of the accident.

You told my own children, that is why you put up with me. What a thing to say but then you were always moaning about me. What did I do wrong? I wasn't an alcoholic or drug addict.

You told all your family I was mad and gave me the reputation as being sex-mad. Why because I was married twice? Even so far as making up a rude song about me that you would sing to everyone at family and friends' partys and get-togethers, How cruel, just so you could get a laugh at my expense. Do you know how that made me feel and still feel now? I remember the song well.

"My Gayley loves cocky, lots and lots of cocky, big ones, brown ones, yellow ones too.

My Gayley loves cocky she doesn't care if their Muslims or Jews."

You belittled me and made me out to be an outcast. I had to live with this slur for all those years. All I ever wanted, Daddy, was your acceptance. I waited all my life to say you were proud of me

The accident and abuse I suffered in the hospital scared me so deeply that even now I suffer with PTSD and recurring nightmares. I went to hell and remember like yesterday the torment I went through. You took me to a Psychiatrist a few years later (not because of what I was suffering, you never had the time or insight to realise that my body and brain had been so severely injured there was bound to be after effects)

Wasn't it you and Mummy who told me the Doctor said that if I survived, I would be a vegetable? What medical term is a Vegetable? Anyway, I thank God that I survived, even though some days have been difficult because of the extreme emotions I feel and depression, but it's because you thought I was mad. You never understood the nightmare I went through every day. I began to feel that maybe you were right, maybe I was mad? Sometimes the thought of killing myself even today would take away the difficulties I have.

For years I could be somewhere, and a dark cloud from nowhere would wash over me and for no reason would cry. I could not stop the tears streaming down my face.

Do you know Daddy, how many years I have been afraid to sleep, absolutely petrified I would be back on the bed in that hospital, paralysed not being able to move? I have never told you or anyone else about it. I took slimming pills to make me feel euphoric and have a zest for life, plus they stopped me sleeping. They were my tablets that I self-medicated myself on and seemed to be the only cure for a happier life. All my senses were heightened, I would feel euphoric and invincible when I took them, but then the irritation and mood swings would set in.

My escape was going out to nightclubs in the night. As I got older, I had to be out as I couldn't breathe being in the confines of a house. In the hospital, I was tied up to chairs with blankets and lying paralysed in the hospital bed not being able to move; it was hell. I would say to myself that if I shut my eyes and opened them again, this would all be a bad dream.

Daddy do you know how many hours, how many nights this occurred. Is it any wonder I suffer from depression, anxiety and claustrophobia? You never tried to understand that being in a coma and taking months off school for rehabilitation to walk and write again took its toll on me. The times I screamed hysterically because of the trauma I suffered.

I was flung over 30 mph up in the air. My skull slammed against the metal lamppost that lined the road. Mummy went to meet me with the dog. As she got closer to the school she saw people gathered around the roadside, she asked what had happened, and someone told her that a pupil from the school had been run over, as she got closer she could see a lifeless body that someone had covered with a jacket, Mummy told me her heart began pounding in her chest as she realised the lifeless body on the ground covered in blood was me.

Thank goodness for my cousins Eric and Caroline who know the real me, after all I lived with them for long enough when I was younger. It was at their parents' home, (my second parents' home in Loughton Essex) Your amazing loving older sister Eva and her lovely husband Benny lived there with their children.

You used to go there every weekend. All the kids, uncles and aunts and cousins used to have a sing-song to the 50s and early 60s records playing on the turntable. You all had to guess the bridge to a song—a truly wonderful musical family. When you told me on many occasions that I had no voice, I sang out of tune. I was unable to gain my confidence back and sing in front of other people even to this day. See, you knocked me down again.

However, others made up for it. My cousin makes up for it with her strong, amazing voice. She should have been a superstar. That is how I remember my family when all your sisters were alive. They kept the family close. Everything was wonderful then Daddy.

You were my wonderful, amazing, loving Daddy that lavished so much love and attention on me your little girl. You would call me your Princess and tell me how beautiful I was and that men will be knocking down the doors to see me. You would think that I would have grown up with such self-confidence, but over the years you cast me aside like a rag doll.

It was a time in my life when I was extremely vulnerable—a teenager who had been in a coma and had to learn to walk and write again. I still suffer with confusion, especially with technical things. I still have memory loss when it comes to numbers and especially now remembering pins and passwords.

I never fully recovered. Mummy told me that at the hospital, she asked me a few times what I wanted to eat, and I said I wanted Bonio, which was dog biscuits. It was hard at first to speak out what I was saying. I wonder if that is why I say what I am thinking when actually I am thinking aloud. My girls say I do that all the time.

It was there in the hall of my Auntie and Uncle's home in Loughton that I got Mummy's phone call. A huge black phone was on the wall. It was the ones that were in the red public phone boxes. It was up on the wall in their hall. There was also a bar, which was very fashionable to have back in those days. You put money in when you called. This was the first type of pay as you go phone.

I remember looking at the wallpaper as I held the black receiver to my ear. I still remember the conversation it is engraved on my mind, as it was life-changing, the same as my life-threatening accident. Not only was I trying to deal with the aftereffects of the accident without counselling-the uncontrollable screams I had, the raw emotions running through my body and the shock that I was very close to death. I had literally been to hell and back.

I had physical damages to my body too. I remember you and Mummy visiting me. Intuitively I remember when I was out of intensive care in the ward. Somehow, I used to try and stand up and see you both walking outside to come and visit me. I used to claw myself up, holding onto the Venetian blinds for dear life. The woman next door told you and Mummy they were injecting me, chemical restraint.

Now, only now am I beginning to understand why every single day I would wake up, but my body was paralysed. It was like my body was locked in, and only my brain was working. Repeatedly I would say to myself this is all a bad dream, when I open my eyes, I will be back home, but that didn't happen. I was locked in my body day after day, buried alive and helpless. I kept trying to scream out for help, but no one ever came because the screams were silent. I know for a fact that my extreme claustrophobia came from that and my anxiety.

Daddy, I couldn't mention that to anyone until about twenty years later. I couldn't tell anyone as even now if I try to recall the absolute worst time of my life, I am back in the living hell. The only way I handled it was going out all the time. Even now, when I am awake, I feel this need to go out from the confines of my house; otherwise, I feel like I am going to suffocate or get a panic attack.

You see Daddy, nobody told this frightened 13-year-old what was happening to her. I was in a coma, the

Doctors thought I would be brain dead when I woke up, but I beat the odds, and I thank God, I survived, but it hasn't been easy for me and a big part of me died that day of the accident. I have had to carry that petrified, broken teenager around with me until this day. The nightmares I suffered in the night caused by my PTSD have kept the memories of me restrained in hospital fresh in my mind. I couldn't tell anyone. In fact whenever the school kids found out they would tell me. "You had head injuries, you are mad, you are mad" they would chant trying to provoke me. My only way of coping was to run away.

When Mummy told me on the phone "Your darling father has walked out on me. He said you should stay there with your aunt and uncle, but I want you home."

All I could do was plead to stay. These were one of the happiest times of my childhood. I wanted to stay here in this house full of love and attention; unfortunately, that wasn't to be.

Daddy when I returned home to Hadley Common, I began to miss you so much. I wanted you here in the house, and so began the dramatic calls, the tears and the cutting of my wrists. I would have done anything to see you again, and in fact, I did. I begged you to come and see me time and time again, but you never did.

I do remember being in your Rolls Royce, and visiting your sisters where all the other family would be. Leaving me at my Auntie Annie's house where your other sisters would come, and we used to go shopping while you and my uncles went off to a football match. As we arrived at the flats in Darenth Road,

Stamford Hill you would whistle the distinct Hiller whistle about 3 times so your sister would know you were there. On the kitchen table was always a mountain of food for us to eat. All your sisters made lovely food. It was so welcoming.

I was still trying to cope alone with the aftereffects of the accident—the uncontrollable fits of screaming, the sadness, the tears. I found life extremely tough. I couldn't cope with any sort of confrontation from the school bullies to unpleasantness at work. If I can't cope with anything, even now, I feel trapped and have to run away from it. That is why I was and am still unable to handle jobs or certain situations. I get so anxious and frustrated, but now my frustration comes out in anger and fear as being aggressive, but that is just to protect myself. When I actually saw you once a month, you used to pick up on every little word I said and give me a lecture. I used to try and change the subject, but if I told you that people agreed with me, you still went on. You always controlled and belittled me.

"I want to know who these people are? Give me their names and phone numbers, and I will call them up." Or another of your classic lines was, "I will call my brother Irving he will know." Haha Daddy, with all due respect to your brother Irving, talented as he was, he wasn't Google. Unfortunately like all of your brothers and sisters, you all had the same attitude to your nieces and nephews. I can hear you now "They are all cunts" or "They are all mad cunts."

That's what you and your siblings used to say all the time about us younger generation. We just never measured up to any of you special people. Unless of course, it was one of the rich nephews or nieces, oh then, they were made out to be so special. It didn't matter that they were alcoholics just as long as they had money it was ok with you. You always had to prove me wrong, and only you and she were correct. Thinking about that now Daddy it was Pathetic, just who did you think you were?

Living with my surrogate family were the most wonderful childhood memories I had. I looked up to my older cousin and happily waited to have her trendy hand me downs. To be in an environment full of love was good for my mind and soul. We used to go to The Dance Centre in Covent Garden. Such great times. Lots of our cousins went too. I used to take two classes, ballet and tap. I remember the clothes everyone wore; it was so trendy. I knitted bell-bottom trousers which I had in navy blue. My granddad top was pink. After classes, we all met up in the canteen and drank Maria's wonderful thick milkshakes.

We are sisters, the closest thing we will have. We were the only girls in the family at one stage. We have experienced so much together. It is a shame that we never saw each other for a few years because you warned her off from contacting me. Maybe you were threatened by her because your usual lie to everyone, of your daughter bleeding you dry was uncovered when she came to the house and saw how the kids and I were living. I still have some of the curtains up that she gave me. Her and David (her husband) went out and bought me a DVD Player and so much more. Caroline was there the day I asked you for a measly £25 as I couldn't afford a bill.

You made so much fuss and refused, yet the family I never saw who never bothered with me ever, thought I was living in luxury because of the lies you told them to make yourself look good, when it was you and her that were going out for meals, attending show business parties, investing in a play and more, while I stayed at home with the kids every night.

I want you to know that I tried to make amends with my brother, but it just never worked out. Like you, he is in awe of your Lady as you always called her. After all, he and his wife always got invited to your house. They have never helped me out with my children, preferring to babysit for cousins instead.

I remember the morning of your funeral. I was sitting outside on the wooden chair in the garden. The sun was shining, but inside of me, I was distraught. The sleeve of my black cardigan covered a cut arm. It wasn't deep, just enough to make me hurt. I couldn't cope with this. I had mourned you years ago, but that was just a rehearsal, this time it was real. In a way it was a relief, no more hurt, no more having to live and compete for your love. To have her ignoring me, the woman you thought was amazing added to my hurt, it was times like these that families were meant to stick together, but we were never classed as family by her.

My wonderful children and their partners were my strength. I had drunk two scotch and cokes for courage. I didn't even want to go. My heart had shattered into pieces. Only one cousin came around to see how I was, when the news that you had died was made public. She didn't tell us until two days before that she had ordered us a cab for the funeral. I tried so hard not to have a panic attack in the locked cab. My kids talked me through it.

When we finally got there, we had to stand outside the chapel until the service began. My children and I stood together. Some people came up and talked to me. When I saw your name written outside the chapel, it became overwhelming.

This was your final destination. Eventually, we all went inside. With everyone seated and some standing up in the chapel of rest, your wooden coffin was in front on the stage. 'United we Stand' was being played. It was hard to believe that you were in that coffin. I half expected you to come walking in with that smile on your face. Memories came flooding back. A lot of music business people wanted to come but couldn't find a flight in time, which is why Eric rightly said that your funeral should be delayed a few more days so you can have the big show business send-off you deserve. Of course, no one listened because they wanted it done ASAP.

In the crematorium, I had to hear a speech made by one of your friends and co-writers that you had worked with for many years. They were one of the biggest successful writing partners of the 60s and also went under the name of Greenaway and Cook. Roger Cook wasn't able to come as he couldn't get a flight in time. Roger Greenaway lived in England and gave a nice speech about you, but then he quoted you, he said that you told him that the best days of your life was meeting her and getting married to her!

It cut like a knife, not a mention of your children or grandchildren or great-grandson. Of course, it had to be all about her. My brother made a speech after about you. I, of course, wasn't even asked. When the service was finished, I wanted to put my hand on the coffin but was whisked away by the female Rabbi and told to stand outside as the mourners were meant to come up to me and wish me long life, hardly anyone did. This was your funeral after all, and I was your daughter. Everyone kept pushing me away and passing me aside, so I got upset, can you blame me, Daddy?

And I told my children I wasn't going to stand like an idiot. In fact, when we went to the garden of peace, more people came and said their condolences. Tony Burrows came up to me. He was in the band called White Plains and Edison Lighthouse, he also sang in the first Brotherhood of Man group. I remember proudly telling him each of my children and their partners' names because that is what parents do. There were lots of other people that I remembered from my childhood days.

Eventually, we got back in the taxi which drove us to your flat. Inside the furniture had been rearranged. The table was covered with food, and still, she and everyone ignored me. Your bedroom door was shut. I had never seen it shut before. During the course of the afternoon, I had three people come up to me and asking who I was? They never even knew you had a daughter. I felt like I was in a stranger's house.

I got a call from my cousin who had flown in from Spain. She told me that she was here to support me. I stood outside the white, painted Victorian flats to greet her. The emotion and feeling like an outcast in my own father's flat, your flat, made me extremely upset. The longer I stayed, the more upset I became. I was hurting really badly. Was this the same place my children and I visited and saw you once a month? I wanted you to walk in and see how I was being ignored.

One of the cousins yelled at me from the other side of the room to sit down on one of the small low chairs as the Rabbi would soon be coming for evening prayers. They were shouting orders at me not even talking to me like a human being.

I sat down, Amber, my daughter, was sitting opposite, and Mitch Winehouse was there standing almost in front of me. Two of your brothers sat down on the left of me. My brother took a seat, two chairs away from me on the right. Nobody said a word; they were talking amongst themselves. It was as if I was invisible. I couldn't take it anymore. I told my daughter that I was leaving. I was shunned in my own father's flat. Imagine that. The memories of all those years we had all spent visiting you were tarnished.

I got up from the chair and said to everyone, "If my Dad were here, nobody would be ignoring me, and you should all be ashamed of yourselves." Of course, she was nowhere to be seen she was hiding away from me, she couldn't bear to be anywhere near me. As I hurriedly walked up the stairs with my daughter, my cousin was having a cigarette outside in the private road, and she asked me where I was going. I began to break down and cry when all of a sudden, another cousin screamed at the top of her voice. "Get back inside now!"

Everyone outside was a witness to this. In hindsight, I understand that she too was filled with emotion and wine. She ran up the stairs and started shouting at the top of her voice. She was abusive to my daughter, who told her not to shout at me like this. Another cousin tried to calm the woman down, but she wasn't having it. She tore into my daughter and then told us that she had to lay the Tallis a Jewish prayer shawl over your Dead body, and asked my daughter Amber if she even knew what a Tallit was? Of course, Amber knows what a Tallit is; she is Jewish.

Her body was shaking, her breath stunk of wine, she was shouting so much, that a neighbour came out on the street and said they were going to call the Police and report a disturbance. My brother came out and after a few words told me to fuck off. My friend, who had just turned up heard the commotion and told the drunk cousin that it wasn't right to behave like this on the street on an occasion like this and in front of your flat. Then the drunken cousin's husband, who is a lawyer, came running up the stairs to drag his wife inside. He was shouting angrily at my friend and me saying that it wasn't your flat Daddy, it was her flat.

He obviously knew about the new will, the one that was changed three years before you died. Did you know about this, Daddy? My daughter and I remained quiet. We did not want to fuel the fire. According to some of the family that had been brain-washed by you for many years, the drama was my fault, well everything was my fault wasn't it?

A few of my cousins begged me to go back inside which I did, she sat next to me with her back turned, as she shared the prayer book with my brother. As the prayers were being said, I hoped that you had seen the whole fiasco and saw how she was blanking me. I seemed to be the only one crying for you at the end.

Eventually, I got up and thanked the drunk cousin for doing everything. I didn't want to leave with bad feelings. The only time she talked to me was to ask me if I wanted a cab. My other cousin had arranged for me to stay with her at her friend's house in Leytonstone.

I was so grateful. I needed her love and support. The same love and support her parents and brothers had given me all those years ago.

We made our way back to her friend's house. He didn't actually know I was coming but was so hospitable. I had no change of clothes just what I was wearing-a plain black dress and new shoes that were a bit too big for me. Her friend made us eat, and as it was a warm summer evening, we sat in the garden having soft drinks and cigarettes trying to make sense of everything, especially the drama.

"You do know," said my cousin, "The family will still blame you for the drama."

Right on cue, your surviving sister rang up and said how disgusting it all was today. My sister had the loudspeaker on as her hands were full and everyone could hear the conversation, I included "You know that Gayle has always been a sick lady." I could not believe what I was hearing.

That is how everyone in the family viewed me. You always spoke badly about me, Daddy. And even if I had difficulties and I had reasons to be the way I was, surely my own father would acknowledge this and protect me? You never bothered to get me any counselling or try to speak with me as you were always too busy. Years later, after telling everyone I was mad the same as you told everyone Mummy was mad when you left her, you sent me to a friend who was a psychiatrist. I also remember being sent to another private psychiatrist who lived in a huge house in Highgate. He was a very rude man. After a few sessions, I never returned.

My cousin and I stayed up and spoke about the funeral all night, we cried, and we laughed until exhausted we both fell asleep just like it was in the old days. I spent another two days there until my cousin returned to her home in Spain. I felt ready to go home and face the children.

I love you Daddy

RIP xxxx

Letter 8

Dear Daddy,

I have written within the constraints of my experiences and memories. I wasn't able to convey my inner thoughts and feelings towards you because money dictated your time and your time dictated your life of which I was deprived of any with you.

Here I am in the garden, sitting in the chair next to the small circular wooden table exactly nine months to the day your cremation took place. I look to the green bushes lining the garden on the right-hand side of the sparse lawn, my mind takes me back to that morning, the morning of your funeral, I remember the sun streaming through the tree's branches and feeling the warmth on my face. The strong whiskey and coke burning my throat as I tried to swallow it, not something, I was used to doing. I was never a drinker, but I had a very emotional day to get through, the kind of day no one wishes to have, even that is actually an understatement, I was actually having one of the worst times ever.

I remember standing on the platform of the train station and contemplating jumping in front of the train.

When you died, I fell apart. I couldn't grieve, I am still at the angry part, but everyone has told me because of how you and she had treated me it is acceptable for me to feel this way—the ultimate betrayal. I really did not want to go to the crematorium because of cruel texts that were circulating about me and one of my daughters. Why one has to be utterly cruel on my father's cremation is beyond me. Only one cousin came to pay their respects to me at home, but then I wasn't close to any of the cousins except for two of them. I have my children and a few close friends. I say hello to everyone, but not a lot of people come to my home as I am a quiet private person.

My arm is no longer hurting from where I cut it. I hid it under a white bandage with a black cardigan on top, I admit that I couldn't cope with your death as it brings up too much hurt from the past. I still can't cope and go through this grieving process. I detest the hurricane of grief that violently whirls within me without a second's notice and mixes up every single emotion. Every single experience past and present goes through my mind. It takes hold of you and is the most intense, saddest, tragic feeling one will ever experience in their life.

I am left in shock and barely able to breathe. The pills the doctor prescribed for me mask the raw, extreme pain. They also make me less emotional, so I do not have to experience this awfully cruel bereavement. Instead, it will just come to me like a dripping tap instead of a tsunami. Sometimes it manages to break through the constraints of the numbness the pills elude. They are extremely good at masking harrowing feelings. They just take the edge of everything.

Nobody knows about the cuts to my arm, except my cousin to whom I showed it to later in the night as I stayed with her at her friend's house. What a lovely man for letting me stay. If only more people were like that. I stayed at his house with my cousin for a few days until she returned home to Spain. She begged me to visit her in Spain. I had not been on a plane for thirty years. I had let my phobias get a hold of me. My darling cousin I grew up with and whom I call my sister was the one person plus the tablets who made it possible. She had begged me for years until she said, 'We are not getting any younger, let's make memories."

When somebody loves you that much, you just have to focus on all the love and positivity. You are dead now Daddy, and even though I am a woman in my late 50s I don't need your opinion or permission anymore, I was finally free from your controlling ways and life was passing me by.

The first air journey I broke down and had a panic attack so bad that I had to be wheeled out in a wheelchair. I managed to compose myself and walk out to where my cousin and her husband were waiting in arrivals. I felt so proud of myself. On the return journey, there was a lot of people that recognised me and told me not to worry. People never cease to amaze me; they can be so wonderful.

I used to go away with my cousin Auntie and Uncle to Spain a lot when I was younger. She is the one who knows me well. She knows the truth behind those wicked comments you used to say to the family.

The white scars are faintly visible amongst my tanned skin, but the scars on my heart go much deeper. I remember the last thing you said to me on your death bed in a room full of people. " I'll always love you." Do you remember saying that?

I loved you so much Daddy and you broke my heart by casting me aside. How I wish you were sitting at the table now, just you and me like it used to be, like it was when you cared about me. How I longed for you and me to be alone, just so we could chat, that's all, for 30 odd years I waited for an opportunity like that, but you never gave me your time. Do you have any idea how that made me feel? You weren't my Daddy then, I just called you 'My Father.' The successful songwriter/producer. It was so important for you to be loved by people in the Music business and strangers, but I was your flesh and blood.

Of course, it wasn't always like that, before she got over your threshold, we used to go out socially together, show business parties, bars, restaurants, at your friends' houses but that all ended abruptly didn't it?

We were all standing at the end of the front garden waiting for the black taxi to take us to the crematorium. The street had all large Range Rovers parked and Mercedes because the neighbour's son was getting married in his grandmother's garden. Their life together was just beginning, which was in stark contrast to your cremation.

As we waited for the taxi, I became proud of my multi-cultural family-my daughter with her Sikh husband, my other daughter whose fiancé was Turkish Kurdish and my son whose father was also Turkish. I was the matriarch. I was the Mother of three wonderful individuals and two lovely men who loved and looked after my daughters plus a grandson who has a special bond with me. I relish the times we go out together. After looking after him for four years, stepping back to let my daughter take over was extremely hard, but I am still his grandmother.

Since your death, most of the family have ignored the children and me. Besides a few of my cousins, not one other person has bothered to see if we are okay. We don't matter, obviously.

She has nothing to do with us and cut us off as if we were dead. What a cruel, nasty woman. Do you still think she is amazing? I know she never liked me, she was jealous that she had to compete with me for your love.

However, she won hands down, she managed to take you away from me. It is not a normal thing to behave like that, this was no competition. I was not another woman; I was your daughter. There was room in your life for me too and your grandchildren.

One of the first things she ever said to me was that when I lived with you, you told her it was supposedly the worst time of your life. Just by telling me this, showed what kind of person she was.

I was ostracized at your Shiva / wake and everyone had rallied around her. It is absolutely heartbreaking; it is like we were not related to you at all. Five people came up to me and asked who I was! Nobody cares about us. and I am unsure about the future, yet we still cry over you, but you do not deserve our tears. You could have helped us. Should I have to be struggling at this time in my life?

Life goes on, regardless. I have and am still going through a hard time. Everything has been exacerbated by your death, but I survived before, and I will survive now.

I look over to the empty wicker chair. The tears are welling up in my eyes as I imagine you sitting in it as a healthy man that you used to be, physically strong in body and mind.

Daddy, I want to ask you that since you have departed this world, spiritually have you witnessed all that has gone on? Are you sorry now, for the comments you made about me?

Every night I am home guarding my children, and home and not one man has been to my house. You used to tell the family I was a scarlet woman, and that is what they all thought. Do you think that was right or a decent thing to do? You slurred my character to the family. You never helped me like other Daddies did for their children because you wanted to be the star—the centre of attention. You were an egomaniac.

Do you see how the children and I love each other and do not live in a house of hate, even your great-grandson tells me how I am the best Nanny in the world. I always have lots of food in the house and make everyone homemade food. I may not be perfect, but I do my best. Isn't that what you used to say? People can only do their best.

You talked terribly about me to your family, what parent does that? You used to lie about me to the family and say I was a thorn in your side, but that was only after you met her. You told everyone you gave me lots of money. You used to take the piss out of me and comment about me to the whole family. How could you do that, Daddy?

Even that same night after the Shiva, I remember it so clearly. It was a very warm evening, and we were sitting around a table in the evening light, talking about the crematorium, You, the events of that day and how I felt sitting on one of the low Shiva chairs and feeling ignored by everyone. The terrible things you said about me stuck with your family, which is why I was never included in a lot of family occasions.

When you and she no longer wanted me in your life, you would tell people I was sick just like you did when you left my Mummy. I hope by reading the truthful letters to you, the family may get to know me better and will not judge me by the cruel comments you made about me. The incorrect picture you built up of me has stuck in everyone's mind.

I would like to see one of them having to bring up one child on their own without a husband, let alone three and have to contend with what I have been through.

Daddy, where are the children you made me abort with you? Yes, that's right, remember Daddy, you and she made me abort these innocent babies because I had to live my life the way you wanted me too, but I am my own woman. I am unique and can only live my life my way. I just wish I had the confidence to stand up to you both, but sadly it has taken your death to get the confidence to let you know what I truly think about you and her.

Daddy, I have waited over half my life to be able to sit and chat with you. The only time we were alone was when you were sedated and hours from death. You were everything to me at one stage. Is it right that a daughter had to fight for her father's attention? Is it right I could not have a relationship with other men because of you? You disapproved of everyone in my life Men woman and even some family members, is it right you discarded me and broke my heart? Is it right a father should make fun of his daughter for his girlfriend's amusement? I remember when you used to embarrass me by singing the vulgar song you made up about me, I was crying inside Daddy, while I watched everyone laughing and her smiling proudly.

We were close at one time, and I lived with you. Just because she got rid of my things does not mean I never existed. We were father / daughter and friends. I was the one you took out as your plus one. I understand you wanted a girlfriend / wife, but why did you have to choose a cold, heartless fish that detested us all? Instead of embracing us all, she split us all up. She tried to keep us at arm's length with our monthly or six weekly visits.

Despite how cruel and unfair you were to me, in fact, the crueller you were to me, the more I seemed to love you. I loved you so much, and you not spending time with me gave me a lot of issues that I still have to work on. I want you to know how much I loved you even though you never gave me your time. When you loved me back, when I was very young, it was the most wonderful time of my life. When I began to see you just once a month, it left me heartbroken. All I wanted was for that love and your time to continue, but it was not to be.

Eight months have elapsed since your passing, my children and I are doing fine. Money is a problem, but we have survived all these years without it, so we're used to living on the breadline. She doesn't want to know us, but did she ever? Nothing has changed there. I don't have to try and gain approval from you anymore, which is a huge relief or feel hurt anymore. In fact, I am free from the confines of criticism, and it has taught me that I don't need approval from anyone as we are doing just fine. I feel that there is going to be a huge change in my life, and I look forward to the future.

I love you Daddy

RIP xxx

Letter 9

Dear Daddy,

Her best friend, one of the cousins by marriage was the one making derogatory remarks about your granddaughter, actually saying that she would steal something from your house absolutely outrageous! Talking lies. This reminds me of the saying ' when the cats away the mice do play.' Why would she have to steal anything from her Pappy's flat. Not only did she poison you against me, she has managed to get other family members on her team.

Amber is such a wonderful daughter; I know you had a soft spot for her, not only is she beautiful like your other granddaughter but deep inside she is a good girl, and I rely on her so much these days. I sometimes think that in the end, you confused us. The way she and her teammates behaved towards us is heartless and cruel! It is not nice for my grandchildren or me. She is the last link we all have to you, father, grandfather and great grandfather. Shouldn't they be allowed into your flat as part of the grieving process? Don't you think they should be allowed that? It is not all about her!

She tried to push us all away, but although our time was greatly limited with you, we still had contact, and you loved us in your strange, selfish, controlling way, I will not let anyone, especially her, tarnish all the memories we spent visiting you even if it was just once a month and by appointment only. She, the one you made out to be so perfect was telling lies about us to her buddies, addressing the witch's coven.

What was she telling them about my family and me, that made everyone have it in for us?? All I can say is that I am so proud of my children and their partners. When I look at them, I know that I have done something good in my life. They are my strength and my family. Struggling as a single parent and a divorcee from a violent man, did anyone of your family ever ask how I was? I have such wonderful memories of how the family used to be when your sisters were younger and alive. It didn't help that I was rarely invited to evenings out, and it was your fault. You didn't include me in anything!

It was so different before when you and I lived together in your Mew's house. Of course, one of the first things she did was get rid of me out of your House What a bitch! She wanted to hurt me and our close relationship. What nasty woman would do that? Daddy why on earth would you let her do this to me? She hadn't broken our strong relationship then as it was still early days, but that was the start of the path she followed, she just carried on with her nasty comments always being rude to me. Daddy did you ever stop and think how this behaviour from her was going to affect me, did you? Or was the spell she had on you so powerful that you didn't even consider my feelings? At the time she was a stranger who was criticising me and our relationship. She probably made snide remarks about me to you. She knew I wasn't going to react because I didn't want any confrontation.

I've never liked confrontation Daddy, that's why I stayed silent for so many years, I preferred to run away and hide. The nasty remarks just kept coming. It began to affect me deeply, and I could see where this was all heading. She wanted me out of your house and out of your life. She even threw out the little pottery figures that I made for you; it's like she wanted every trace of me gone from your life.

Eric told me, Daddy, that during this time you and she said to him that as he and I get on so well it would be great if I could live with him. Of course, as much as Eric loved me, he really was used to living on his own and didn't want a flatmate. However, because she wanted me out I did end up staying with Eric for a month, I also bagged a job at one of the hotels in Sussex way. I did tell you, but you were so wrapped up in her you didn't care. Eric lived nearby in Star Street.

My first shift at the hotel was the night shift. I can't say I remember my shift, but I do know that I was so tired, and the Manager of the hotel was an Irish man with a rather thick accent and large black moustache. He said that I could have my break and have a little sleep in one of the vacant hotel rooms. It had a huge bed against the wall and as soon as my head touched the plump pillows, I fell asleep. My sleep was interrupted by the door which had been slammed shut and walking over towards the bed was the manager. He sat on the bed beside me and attempted to kiss me, yuck!

I asked him what he was doing. I was absolutely shocked. After grappling with him for around 5 minutes, I managed to get up and collect my things. I screamed at him, and he knew I was not letting him get his way. Needless to say, I never returned to that job again. I was too embarrassed to tell Eric what had happened.

The showbusiness parties I attended with you were full of well-known people. I remember going to the London Palladium with you. On the next table was Princess Margaret, the Queen's sister. I remember glancing over to where she sat and out of her evening bag, she took lipstick and applied it. She never followed protocol and excused herself to apply lipstick in the privacy of the ladies. I thought that was brilliant and a bit puzzled after all in those days we all had to be seen to follow rules.

So that is what I did. If it was good enough for Princess Margaret, then it was good enough for me. I remember going to a lot of parties with you and Eric Hall. After all, it was Eric who worked with you in ATV Music. Not only that, but he was your nephew and friend. You two were so close, but she didn't want him coming around to the flat neither.

Something I always wanted to ask you Daddy: You used to talk about me behind my back to the whole family branding me very promiscuous was it because you found out at your birthday party in Serafinos that I had slipped away with one of your showbusiness friends?

I was a young teenager and was very impressionable. The bar was absolutely jam-packed. Your friend was a lot older than I was and extremely good looking.

He had the most amazing appearance. Those piercing brown eyes and film star looks were so appealing.

I had heard that he was a singer and had released many records. Even though he was so much older than I was, I was very flattered when he caught my eye and came over to me. We started talking, and I felt very flattered to have his attention. There was an immediate attraction. He made me feel that there was only him and I in the room. He bought me lots of drinks, mainly wine. I began to feel tipsy.

He was over six foot and made me feel very special. I remember telling him I felt tipsy and he suggested going somewhere else. I followed him up the stairs, and he ended up taking me to some posh hotel, I think it was in Chelsea.

When we sat on the hotel bed, he told me that I was so attractive. I remember I was wearing a black velvet jacket. He moved further towards me and began to kiss me-a real kiss from a real man that I had never had before. Being experienced, he took off my black velvet jacket, and as the alcohol I drank began to consume me, he seduced me. I had never felt this way before.

As we both lay on the crisp white sheets, I felt so wonderful. We talked after, and I remember him bragging about all the female singers and actresses he had bedded. He was very confident and full of himself. We never saw each other again.

I will always remember that wonderful experience.

A couple of years ago I saw him on TV. Of course he was much older and grey, but still an attractive man, looking good in his colourful shirt. It was a show where celebrities were flown to Las Vegas to perform on stage there. Also, around the same time, he did a big article in a National Newspaper, stating that he and his wife had been married for 50 years, and he had never been unfaithful to her, Well, that's not true, he slept with me.

I remember when you found out Daddy. You were absolutely livid. You didn't care that your friend had seduced me, that was okay with you. Apparently, it was all my fault. I was the one who led him astray you told me. Ever since then you branded me a nymphomaniac and was happy to tell all the family. That was when you made up songs about me. That was when you tarnished me. In my family's eyes I always had a reputation that never went away. What kind of a father were you to do this to me?

Do you remember when you told me off again, at another showbiz do, as another show biz friend of yours was talking to me? I could see you out of the corner of my eye, running toward me as if in a panic, you grabbed my arm and you pulled me aside and said aggressively that I shouldn't be talking to him because his wife was seated close by. Haha haha. Was I not allowed to speak with anyone of your friends because he was married? Absurd. He was an elderly man and did most of the talking. I was just being polite because he was your friend. Maybe I should have ignored him.

Did you think, Daddy, that just because I had slept with your friend a couple of weeks earlier when in fact it was your friend who seduced me and took advantage of a young, innocent teenager, that I was going to sleep with all of your friends? How ridiculous you really were.

I Remember Daddy how me you and Eric used to go to lots of show business parties. There were always well-known faces at the parties. I remember going to one where Marc Bolan was, and we were speaking bizarrely about Elvis Presley, his death and Marc told me how much he admired Elvis. Funny, but months later I found out Marc had been killed in a car accident.

Going out to restaurants with you, we always saw a famous face. Once we were eating out at a trendy restaurant and Elton John was there. Wasn't he the office boy when you worked in Mills Music in Denmark Street and wasn't he the singer that did the demo for you of 'United we Stand?' Plus, David Bowie worked opposite as an office boy? The famous Tin Pan Alley.

The 80s, in my opinion, was one of the best times in pop music. There were some great camp groups around like The Sweet, Bay City rollers, Wizard, Showaddywaddy. Being camp and bisexual went with the image of the eighties, especially the singers. At one party, I was propositioned by the partner of Mike Mansfield. He told me he was bi-sexual, but I was in no way interested. I was a young heterosexual female.

If I were your son, you would have encouraged me as your views were always a bit sexist. I should never have been the butt of your jokes. Did you want me to feel cheap? I don't know why you had to comment to your family and try and make me look and feel bad all the time, did you do it to make yourself feel good or was it to keep her happy.

To be honest with you, Daddy, sleeping with men was the nearest thing I got to feeling loved. You, walking out on us all, had such a devastating effect on me. The attention I got from men made up for all those times I never saw you. I loved the attention from males. Unfortunately, I mistook sex for love.

After I returned from living abroad, I used to go to London clubs. At that time there were a load of Arab men and they all smelt of Aramis. It's funny the things I remember now. They were lovely people and made me feel so special. I loved going out to night-clubs. I couldn't drink a lot because of the diet pills I was taking- controlled amphetamines. Sometimes I would take a double dose to keep myself up. I had so much energy and a black cab from central London to Cockfosters was a lot of money, so sometimes I never took a cab home. My friend and I would go to an all-night restaurant. We would wait there until the first train in the morning. I remember meeting John Conte, the boxer ,and going for a drink with him. He was always going on about Jesus.

After drinks at the hotel, we went for a pub crawl and ended up in The Hog and Pound pub that used to be on the corner of South Molten Street- one of my favourite streets. I was never into drinking much, and by then it was almost midday, so we parted company. I never saw him again and remember reading many years later that he had a serious health problem caused by too much drink.

You know Daddy, I lived for those days. I should have carried on clubbing. I don't know why I stopped. I was one of the first IT girls. Life was so exciting then. After that time, my life became mundane. I was definitely destined for better, brighter things. After those wonderful times, nothing could replace them. Living in bedsits and working in different jobs was extremely tough and brought me down to earth. I couldn't handle any of the jobs, and the anxiety of being on a three-month trial ruined my chances of staying permanently in any job. When you were away on business, leaving me alone in the house, I was out every night. I wasn't going to stay in alone and be miserable.

At that time, I was going to Corona Stage School in Hammersmith. Nicholas Lyndhurst was there and already in a TV series. He always wore a blue anorak same as another actor who went on to star in the TV series Emmerdale, can't remember his name though. I used to feel inadequate going there as all the girls were skinny and I was big.

You and your family had a thing about weight. You were always mentioning it. That is another form of controlling someone. So, I made myself Ill by going on all these ridiculous diets. Give me diet pills, and I could do two high-intensity aerobic classes. The only regret I have is going to another country. If I hadn't, she wouldn't have got under your skin and taken over, and maybe you would have found someone so much nicer, better.

You should have stayed with the Lebanese woman; she was so nice to me. She treated me so nicely when she came over to stay with you. Do you remember how we always went out together and it was like a happy family. Why couldn't we have stayed a happy family?

I love you Daddy

RIP xxx

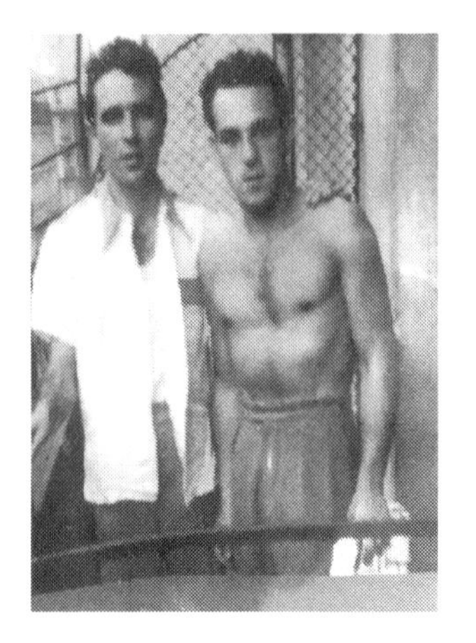

My Father the boxer, 1940s. Tony Hiller (right) was on his way to becoming a professional boxer, but his father Sam did not want him to continue.

When we were a family: a Hiller family photon taken by a professional photographer.

Me and my daddy. It broke my heart that we could never spend quality time together when I returned from living abroad.

Eurovision Award Winners: The Brotherhood of Man won the contest with the song, "Save All Your Kisses for Me," in 1976. Two days later, Tony Hiller left the family home, breaking my mother's and my hearts.

My father at home, taken on one of our monthly visits, 2017.

At the radio station, Time FM. During an interview on the Eric Hall show with Mitch Winehouse, Father of Amy Winehouse, who's holding my portrait of Amy.

After I asked for a year, in 2019 my father's second wife allowed me to have a few of his Gold Discs.

My two precious stones, my daughters Amber and Jade. I think they both look sweet in this photo.

I am also blessed to have a wonderful son. This was taken in Wales in 2016. My children and I spent many a summer holiday staying with my late friend Maggie.

A rare photo of my Father and my son. My Father never gave him any time yet my son looked up to him.

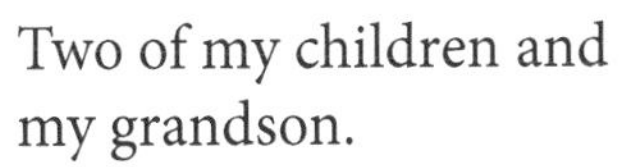

Two of my children and my grandson.

Me and my mummy, 2019. I admire her for her strength and how she coped with my father walking out. In a way, we were both casualties of Tony Hiller.

At my mum's house, where we celebrate every Christmas.

My Aunt Eva, who was a second mother to me. She often took me to writer's workshops and poetry readings.

My cousin Caroline Stevens who I call my sister, my confidante. Taken at the beach when I visited her at her home in Spain.

Stormzy in front of my painting. He and the producer were alerted to it as it was displayed in the cafe in the Hugh Corbett Center near where the video for his song Blinded by Your Grace was filmed.

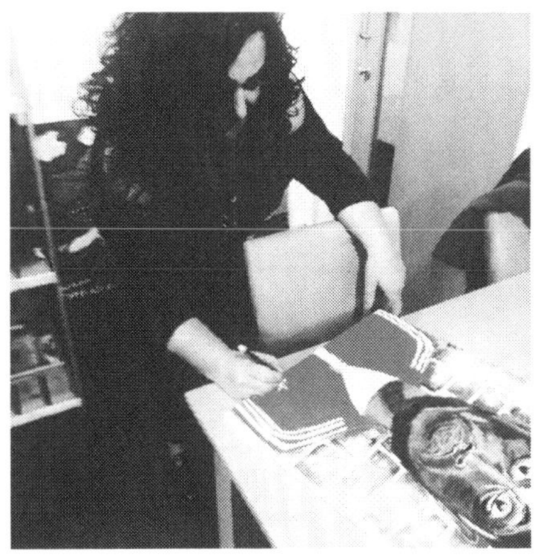

I was asked to come down to The Hugh Corbett community centre and sign my painting of Stormzy, as The Director of his music video said he wanted to buy it for Stormzy as a momento of the day.

Letter 10

Dear Daddy

It has been over a year since you passed away. The emotions are still very raw, a gaping wound that refuses to heal and grows even bigger fuelled by past memories. The realisation that you weren't this wonderful family man you made yourself out to be to others. If truth be known, I have been grieving for years, probably since the day you walked out on us and then again when she came into your life and I'm still grieving. Daddy, I thought you loved me so much, but then you cast me aside once you had found her. I have had to fight for your love and attention for most of my life. In a way, I am relieved I don't have to punish myself anymore by trying to always gain your approval.

You will always be known as the successful songwriter/producer of over 2,000 hits, better known as the manager/producer of The Brotherhood of Man and co-writer of the biggest selling Eurovision song of 1976 with 'Save your Kisses for Me.'

It was number 1 in over 40 countries-even making the Billboard Charts in America.

Since you died Daddy, I have been reading a lot about the Eurovision song contest. There is so much I didn't know; I didn't know that there was an organisation for fans in every country in Europe and even Australia, absolutely millions and millions of Eurovision fans all over the world.

I started a Facebook page, and the minute I joined one of the fan pages it hit home to me how successful 'Save your Kisses for Me' really was and still is, the fans still say it's the best Eurovision song ever, most memorable for not just the song, but the dance too. This is the legacy you have left behind Daddy, but not for me, there will be **No more Kisses for me.**

Your death has affected us all. The children and I are all trying to cope in our own way. I haven't been able to deal with the grief. The other issues I have are exacerbated by this grieving process which has bought on a depression. I wonder if it is depression or just grief? It's confusing. The bottom of my world good or bad has been snatched away from underneath my feet, and I have been tiptoeing through the days, scared to put my feet firmly on the ground as if I do the tsunami of grief will get a strong grip of me again and hold me to ransom for days maybe even weeks and I am unable to cope with it. I choose to escape and take anti-depressants which leave me in a relaxed, sleepy state. It is too painful to feel any kind of grief. I am a strong lady, a one-woman army, my friends call me, but I refuse to fight this battle. I prefer to curl up on the sofa and let sleep take over my troubled mind. I want to be in this safe cocoon forever.

Today Tyrone your grandson and I had an early morning appointment with the headmaster of his school which turned out to be a blessing in disguise. I stressed myself out before the meeting. My overthinking getting the better of me. I think it was you, Daddy, who is really to blame for my worrying overreacting neurotic behaviour sometimes.

Tyrone your grandson doesn't show his emotions, but if you had read the eulogy, he wrote for you then you will understand exactly what he thought of you. It is heart-breaking that your own grandson you never gave your time to, is suffering, would you have done things differently if you knew this?

You were too busy trying to impress others and her, but Daddy, we are your flesh and blood. You were a selfish man and never gave your time as a grandfather, because you were too busy with yourself or her, your second wife.

When we used to visit you on our monthly visit, Tyrone sat and waited a long time as you didn't really speak to him much. I feel sorry for him that he didn't have a strong male character in the family that was active with him and took him under their wing. Tyrone and I used to be extremely close, and he would ask me to take him out to the cinema at the weekends and visit places, we had lovely memorable days out together.

Where were you Daddy? Did you ever take any of your Grandchildren on a day out? The Seaside for the day? No, you never did, and why not? It's sad that none of your grandchildren will have memories of days out with you to tell their children. When Tyrone turned 15, I used to encourage him to go out with friends instead of me. I thought I needed to cut the apron strings but this had a worse effect as he would be in his room on the X Box that his father bought for him probably out of guilt, as he disappeared for over two years from his son's life, not that he was an active father anyway. Although he is trying harder now.

Remember Daddy, Tyrone's father walked out on me when he was a baby. I was broken-hearted, but my love and care for my son and his sisters kept me going. His grandparents Mum and her partner lived only a few doors away would see us through. Did I ever tell you Daddy that Tyrone's father would often call me and be angry that his son never called him Daddy? I explained that one has to earn that name. A bit of money here and there can never compensate for giving your time. Does that ring a bell with you? Exactly the same as you, Daddy! Coming from a large family always talking about the good old days, I thought that would have made you more involved with your own family. How wrong was I?

For a long while now whenever I used to ask Tyrone to go out it was an impossibility as he never woke up until the afternoon and by then I had been out all morning and was pleased to then stay in the house. I always tried to make homemade food in the evening. And I needed time for the preparation and cooking to be ready by 5 pm because at that time the kids and I were all hungry.

Do you know how hard it has been as a single parent? But I wouldn't change it for the world as I feel blessed. When I see all my children together and my grandson, I feel so proud. I know that I got that right. You wanted me to abort all my babies and forced me to abort two. You said if I didn't that you would have nothing to do with me. You wouldn't care if I was on the streets. "You won't get a penny from me." Remember Daddy? You said it nastily, and what happened? I didn't get anything from you anyway.

On our once a month visits you would give us a few quid just enough to pay for our family of 5 train and bus return tickets to visit you, yet you made out you were such a great family man. Well, let me tell you what I have been wanting to tell you for the last 30 odd years, "You weren't nowhere near the best family man, in fact, you were one of the worst."

I have been there for all my children; one can only do their very best-staying in each evening, planning exciting things to do, not getting a break because evenings out were too expensive.

Daddy, you never once offered to take any of my children out. You weren't like other grandfathers. The only time you called up was to inform me of the date that was convenient for you and her to see us. It was the same conversation every month.

Remember Daddy what you used to say, "Put the 25th down, you and the kids are coming here" But if I couldn't make it on the day that suited you, I would have to wait two months to see you.

That's how it was Daddy. We just existed, of course, you knew we were there in the land of the living, but we were so unimportant to you, we were all nothing to you and her.

What father, grandfather has to look in their diary to see if they can see their daughter and his grandchildren? You always made time for her cousins or friends who visited from Australia. We weren't important enough. Once I actually told you about other grandfathers and fathers who saw their family every week regularly.

You replied in your condescending way, "Yes, I know I am a bad father and grandfather." You used to joke about it when in actual fact that was the truth. I feel confident to tell you that now, of course, I couldn't before.

Whenever there were school holidays, I would suggest it would be nice to see you then, but that was just too normal for you. That never happened. You never took my feelings into account, No, Daddy, we weren't worthy of a holiday, but when one of your granddaughters and I were visiting you and were around your bed as you lay dying and sedated, we had to hear her friend thank you for all the holidays you paid for, for her and her children. My daughter and I just looked at each other in shock. How do you think it made us feel on hearing this? How Disgusting you were.

When we arrived at Tyrone's school for the meeting with the headmaster, he was very welcoming. He took us into his office and once seated around a circular light wooden table I noticed the desk with the huge computer screen on it, he pointed to a piece of paper. Tyrone's grades were well below average, and he asked him why this was. Tyrone was capable of good grades which earned him a place in the top classes.

The Headmaster, a very caring person, wanted to find out why his grades of 7 had fallen to 3. Did he not understand the work? Why did he not ask a teacher for help?

Eventually, I interjected and called it Mother's intuition, but I just blurted out, that since his grandfather had died last year, he has just locked himself away in his bedroom and played on his X Box, shutting the world outside. His eating and sleeping patterns had just gone to pot.

On hearing me say these words, mentioning you Daddy, Tyrone started crying uncontrollably. To see him sob his heart out was the saddest thing I had witnessed. A Mother is a lioness that wants to protect her Cubs even when they grow older. Tyrone had tragically lost a school friend that he was close to a year before. In hindsight I should have got him counselling then. It was the Easter holidays, the very same time as I am writing you this letter. When he returned to school after the Easter break, his friend didn't.

I put my arm on his shaking shoulders and told him to let it all out. He mentioned his friend whom the Headmaster was well aware of, and I believe Tyrone's tears were also for her. Daddy, you never deserved all those tears, your interaction with your grandson was minimal, yet you made such a huge impact on his life, and in fact, your death has affected him an awful lot. We both cried in the office, and the headmaster understood his pain and loss. I took a large tissue out of the box which never ripped off, and the table was awash with white. The white tissues that absorbed me and my sons' tears. If only they could have absorbed and rid us of this hurt. This huge hurricane that appears out of nowhere and whirls into the core of your very being.

Every nerve, every emotion, is affected to the point of physical exhaustion and pain. Grief is hidden away in this Western society. One can barely look at a shop which provides burials, and we walk past extremely fast. We believe we are immortal; we collect money and material things believing they will act as a barricade against death. Even the great Kings and Queens are not immune. Death is nothing to be afraid of, it is part of the circle of life but because of our refusal to acknowledge it, when someone who was part of your life passes over, we are left in torment like the huge elephants that mourn the passing of a loved one. Ashes to ashes, dust to dust.

Daddy, you were certainly in no way the doting grandfather, but you were the only grandfather he had, so I put my hand on his shoulders, that moved up and down with the sound of his tortured sobs.

The headmaster went to get us two plastic cups of water. Will water wash away the after effect of a tortured soul?

I looked at my baby boy, sobbing. I touched his arm. "It's okay, my Darling, let it all out.'

The headmaster took my son to see a counsellor in the school straight after the meeting. He had shown my son so much attention and compassion in that short time, much more than you had ever shown him in his lifetime.

As a Mother, you don't want to see your child unhappy. You want to protect them. At the beginning, when I was texting her a little, I explained that the children were very upset and would like to see her. Did she think it was only her grieving? I don't think it even crossed her selfish mind!

Your death has affected us all. We have all been trying to cope in our own way, yet she has cruelly denied us of going to your home. The kids won't even go to Edgware road or Marble Arch anymore because of the memories of you. I remember telling you Daddy that after we saw you, we would walk from your flat up to Edgware road where Tyrone would be eager to buy something from Argos. Something he or your other Grandchildren won't be doing again because we are not welcome by her.

Daddy did you know how much Tyrone thought of you. We don't mention anything about you, or any of the pain around our Little Harvey, as he told his Mummy, when she was crying, not to be sad as it was okay because you were now in heaven with the angels. Well, Are you?

Love you, Daddy

RIP xxx

Letter 11

Dear Daddy,

I am daydreaming again; I tend to do that a lot lately. I'm back in my bedroom in Hadley wood. The sun is trying to shine through the bright yellow curtains that are drawn in my bedroom. I can see you in my mind's eye-opening them up and the sun flooding the room. You always came in singing, which woke me up. 'It's a lovely day today, the birds are singing." I found that so annoying you would get annoyed that I never greeted you in the way you wanted in fact I think I would tell you to go away, quite normal for teenagers to act this way but the way you went on is like I had committed a heinous act.

Talking to you through these letters has made me aware of the kind of Mother I want to be. How being a parent has a profound effect on children? It is a huge responsibility bringing up a child to be a decent human being. It starts with the parents. You know, Daddy, you always told me to tell my children I love them every day. Whenever I called you up on the phone you would always tell me that you loved me, but they were just words like you were reading them from the script that was in front of you, but in real life, you never gave us your time.

There was no truth or sincerity as you spoke words of love. It just hurt me that you, my Daddy was so unattainable and that gave me such deep sorrow. I could only converse with you on the phone before she told me not to call you. It was your house and music company, but she would pick up your phone. She was Hyde Park Music apparently. You were always telling me how wonderful she was. I never quite found out what she actually did except tell you what to wear, eat and drink and who you could see, and they were only the people she wanted around, however me, and my children were not.

My boys are so loving and tell me they love me every 30 minutes just in case I forget. Amber always tells me at the end of her texts. Jade tells me she loves me too. The love you poured on me when I was younger was so generous and strong. It comforted me to have had that love even though I had to fight for it when you walked out on us and then let her into your life.

Today I tried to wake up Tyrone. He has a lock on his door. Every morning I have to bang on the door to wake him up. All he has to do is come to the door, so I can see he is up, but he doesn't, so instead I get really anxious, my heart starts pounding. There are mornings when I have to literally tear myself away from the bed in a trance-like a sleepy state.

I fight this tiredness every single day. I have to sleep by 9 pm. I am always in a state of tiredness bought on by the anti-depressants. Daddy, I do not know if they are truly working as lately, I have just been crying. I can't mention your death to anyone as the sad, desperate, heartbroken tears just start sliding down my face and I can't shake this desperate sadness off. I am not coping well with it. I don't suppose there is a pill to numb myself? A pill that will make me devoid of any feelings?

Every single emotion I felt for you, the heartache and sadness, of her creeping into your life with that false Cheshire grin working her evil witchcraft on you but is she really to blame after all you allowed it. My senses are heightened a thousand times as these feelings come back to haunt me. Those dire, dark days that I had to endure, Daddy, as I saw her pull you away from me. I was unable to do a thing just let it happen. You don't know how scared and tear-stained my heart is.

My anxiety always gets the better of me. Why hasn't Tyrone left the house, what if he is late for school? A million what-ifs fill my head that I have to get out the house that is enclosing me. I need fresh air to breathe, after one hour and I am just beginning to be able to breathe easy again. I don't think the coffee is helping. I am worried I will get so worked up one of these days I will have a heart attack,.Tyrone needs a deposit of £50 to go on a trip but if I give him that, I will have no money left.

I will tell him that unless he improves with getting up in the morning for school, I won't give him the money (but of course, I will). I am just so thankful that he has found something that ignites passion within him. This is his lifeline, and I thank God for this.

I told you, Daddy, he is having bereavement counselling. He has all but given up on his studies. I told him that you would be proud of him if he did well in his exams, however, I don't really think he believed me or that you would care, as the most important people were you and her. You never boasted about your grandchildren. Well how could you when people never even knew you had a daughter? We were kept hidden in the background. She wanted to stake her claim on you, and she certainly did that. What an investment she has got. Sitting comfortably on millions of pounds worth of property while the kids and I suffer, but I will not let my spirit be defeated. Where there is life, there is hope.

Tyrone doesn't want to go to university now but who can blame any young person from feeling this? After all nobody wants to be in debt at the beginning of their working life.

He shouldn't really shed tears for you as you really don't deserve them. You never gave him time. You promised he would have a bar mitzvah, but as usual, you went back on your word. You told me that it would be too much money. Well I am not sure now, if he is at all interested in religion. He believes in God. He has a non-practising Jewish Mother although the one thing I like to do is light the Sabbath candles as it keeps me connected and of course I pray every day. I pray that I will be a good mother and grandmother and be a better version of myself.

I can emphatically say that there is a higher power, and even though a part of me died after the car accident, I am grateful for each new day.

You never believed in God or religion. You told me that in later years but I don't think that was true. You were not religious in the sense of going to synagogue, but you stood up for Jews most of your life. Everyone was surprised that you had a cremation—one more thing you did to please her.

I will always remember the summer of 2018. It was a scorcher. I remember because you were very ill with your liver cancer. It saddens me a great deal that the only time she allowed me and my children to see you more than once a month was when you were dying. I was given a time to come which my daughters and I would adhere to. We would have to catch the train which would be a 40-minute train ride. We would usually be early and spend time in the coffee shop around the corner to your flat.

She would say that as it was a nice sunny day, we should go to Hyde Park that was not far away. You weren't always enthusiastic about going out, and it would take a long time to get you ready. You had lots of tubes coming out of your body because of the stents. Once she was painstakingly trying to put your shoes on, as she didn't want you to go out in slippers, so I told her that your M&S slippers looked fine, besides you were in a wheelchair.

It was hard to see you supported trying to step down from the entrance and navigate the stone steps that led onto the street. This was very hard for you. Trying to get you seated in the wheelchair was another mammoth task. You didn't even have the strength to pick up your legs. Eventually, we all went to Hyde Park pushing you in your wheelchair. It was basically straight across the way; it was only about five minutes from your flat. She put a ridiculous cap on you that if you were well mentally, you never ever would have worn.

To see a lion of a man reduced to being in a wheelchair was heartbreaking. Once when I was pushing you in the wheelchair, you asked if I had a husband?

"No Daddy, I haven't now," I replied. No one could compare to you, I thought. The love and attention you gave me as a child set the precedence. To then have that love you have always known ripped away from you when you are vulnerable and need your loving father was something I have not got over even to this day. We used to have lunch in the cafe in Hyde Park, you of course never ate.

To think you had a most voracious appetite all your life. All this pressure to diet in this society makes no sense. We lose weight when we are ill. On most occasions, outside the cafe overlooking the Serpentine, the wooden tables and chairs were occupied, we would find a table and chairs inside.

Do you know what Daddy? Tyrone has been grieving all year for a man he only saw once a month. Did you think the little treats a tenner here and a tenner there you gave him when you were alive would compensate for your time? However, that is all he knew from you. To be honest with you, Daddy, the girls are absolutely disgusted that you never provided for them in your will.

Also, the pain that they have been going through because she, the only remaining link to you, has totally wiped them out of her life. Although she gave Tyrone some glimmer of hope when she sent him a birthday card and suggested that if he was ever around her area to contact her. Tyrone was really pleased to hear from her and immediately phoned her to arrange a meeting to which she replied she was away, and he hasn't heard from her since.

Mummy's partner does more for Tyrone, He does all the things granddads should do, and although he can be a bit overpowering, he does It because he cares.

At the crematorium service, I asked my brother, your son, if Amber and Tyrone could each read out their eulogy but was told the eulogies had all been arranged, and they were not allowed. So, you see Daddy, even in Death me and my children were not included, not to feel part of it, and really, they had more right than anyone else, after all, they were your flesh and blood. As Tyrone wasn't allowed to read out the Eulogy at your Funeral, I want to let you know what Tyrone wrote for you. So finally, you might understand how your Grandson loved you. Although you never loved him in return.

"I don't like sharing personal matters in public, but this man was the most important man in my life. My Grandfather, Tony Hiller, has always been my idol since I was a little child. He was raised in the tough East End of London with nothing, but through hard work and dedication, he made a life for himself. He had a band called The Brotherhood of Man, and he won the Eurovision. He was my idol, my everything. Every single time I saw him he would smile and laugh and sing his heart out, he had the voice of an angel and the personality to bring light even in the darkest of days. He was the greatest man in my life, always telling me I could do anything always inspiring me to work hard and do more. I loved him so much. At heart, he was a fighter the strongest I've ever known. He was the kindest smile in a room of frowns and the fiercest flame in the coldest of winds, no one in my life can compare to my Grandfather he told me you're here 5 minutes on this earth, so you have to

make the most of it and make your mark. Well, you did that Pappy you made your mark not only on me but everyone who knew you. I love you Pappy. I pray now that you are in a better place where you can smile and sing all you want. You will forever be in my heart, and you will be sorely missed in the hearts of everyone who knew you. I love you so much, rest in peace my beloved Pappy."

So, Daddy, how do you feel about that? Did you deserve this amount of love and respect from your Grandson? I'm afraid I don't think so.

At the Shiva house, one of the cousins made a speech about you, but instead of speaking about you he decided to use the opportunity and occasion to embarrass me and your granddaughter Amber and spoke of one of the hardest times in my life, when Amber went missing. I never ate until they found her I don't believe it was his right to bring that up; why, why, why? Again, was it to make me look bad as a person or as a Mother, plus it was absolute rubbish to say you were walking the streets looking for her. You had no idea where she was.

In fact, if the truth be known, the day after or two days after she had not returned home, the police were at my house. Do you know I was so distraught that I got into the car, I was an absolute emotional wreck, and as I turned on the ignition Jade flung herself onto the car bonnet to stop me from moving as I was threatening to kill myself? I felt like driving at high speeds to try and get rid of my utter helplessness and sadness. I felt like driving with all my emotions into a brick wall. I could not see a way out of this. My baby hadn't come home. It is every mother's nightmare.

I remember one of my friends asking me at midday on the second day, "Where's your father?" As usual, you hadn't bothered to come and see me and comfort your distraught daughter and see how the other children were. It was always like this, and I thought it was normal. It wasn't till I saw other grandfathers visiting their children nearly every week or every day if they lived close that I knew I had been missing out and the lack of your presence was causing me heartache. Especially as we used to be so close.

When you and she finally put in an appearance at my house, you were of no help at all, and for the first time, I saw the Detective who was in charge actually stand up against you and told you not to talk to me like that, as you were only making me agitated.

How could anyone dare argue with you, the great Tony Hiller? I could not believe it, after all everyone bowed down to you. My goodness, someone in a higher power than you actually stood up against you. I was absolutely dumbfounded! That put you in your place. That evening, thank God, they eventually found her. Nothing comes as close to a mother's heartbreaking.

I love you Daddy

RIP xxx

Letter 12

Dear Daddy,

I woke up today as I do every morning and thanked God for a beautiful sunny day, my children and my life. Of course, my discovering I could paint only two years ago was a gift from God. I waited until then to hear that you were proud of me. I used to think that if I was in a long-term relationship, you would be proud of me, but I know now that was an impossibility because of you.

You see Daddy, by you leaving me twice any man that I would be with, any chance of happiness I was feeling, was only temporary. I was somehow addicted to happiness and heartache and so set the precedence for my love life. I never ever wanted to be abandoned again and I couldn't put myself through that, not forgetting the injuries from the car accident. The mental scars and torture I went through stayed with me all my life. That petrified girl remained a part of me, clinging on deep within my body and mind.

The one time I needed security and love from you and Mummy, you were both busy with each other, and I was overlooked. I stopped believing in fairy tales and happy ever afters a long time ago.

Today I had to walk 2.9 miles in sandals that burnt my feet. I didn't have any money on my debit card, and my oyster was missing, probably one of the kids took it, but I don't care. That is what families do.

I just told Tyrone not to eat the sausages as that is for our evening meal which I shall make with one of my delicious omelettes. It's a good job. I know how to cook, a must when one has a family. It was my Auntie Eva, your sister that told me if you have eggs and potatoes in the house you will always have a meal, I think she took that advice from your mother, whose whole life was devoted to cooking for her large family.

Sometimes I imagine I am on that cookery programme with Ainsley Harriot when you are given certain ingredients to make a meal. It is quite challenging, but then that is my life. Most days are a challenge for me. Of course, I am trying to change my life, but there are family commitments, and as much as I want to try and better me and the children's lives, I am not a selfish parent like you were. If only I was able to make my children's lives so more comfortable, but then they are all doing fine.

Dinner was delicious Daddy, and better still Tyrone had bought sweets for dessert. Harvey told Amber that he didn't want to stay with her at Mummy's. He said he wants to stay here with me because as a baby he was always with me and he misses going out with me. When Amber was ready to take over as a mother, I had to step back, I did it, but it was not easy. I sort of lost my way a bit. I was at a crossroads in my life, but just at that time, things fell into place.

However, it was doing arts and crafts with my grandson that I discovered I could paint. The bond between my grandson and I is very strong and special.

He said he loves living here because of the animals, Tyrone (a brother from another Mother) and a beautiful kind Nanny. That made me cry; it was so touching. A reality check that I am loved.

We may not go out to fancy restaurants like you and she did all the time as I am always juggling money but to hear that from my grandson made me feel like the richest woman in the world. You see Daddy, you were always going on about your family in the past, but you never replicated that in your life. You missed out on so much. I understand that showbusiness was exciting, and everyone had a piece of you—everyone except your immediate family. Ultimately you were the loser.

I was thinking of moving, but your grandson is going to be sitting A levels, and he doesn't want to move. The counselling has really had a good effect on him, and he is going out more with school friends. I am so happy for him, although I feel I would be happier if I had a car to drive him to friends and pick him up. He knows I get really anxious so he will call me to tell me when he is coming home, and I will speak to him on his journey back. He will be 17 soon, Daddy. A young man in his own right. A big strapping lad with a full beard and moustache, but he will always be my baby.

When he went to school to get his GCSE results, I could not contain myself any longer as I was worried about him passing Maths. I phoned him up, and when I heard he had passed every exam and got some top marks, I burst out crying for joy. It hasn't been easy for him, but he did it. The same as Jade, his older sister did, who then went on to university.

I suppose your lady will be eating out with her friends or some of the family, who think I am living it up. Hahaha. If only they knew the truth. Do these people not have a conscience? I suppose not.

As I had a dentist appointment, I headed straight to the parade and rested my body in a chair in the coffee shop. I found £2.85 in loose change at the bottom of my handbag plus I could use their internet. My whole body just melted in the chair. I don't realise sometimes that I am older now.

The very last of my money went on a packet of cigarettes. They are the one thing I enjoy. No, I am not giving them up.

You know what Daddy. My life is a far cry from being the daughter of Tony Hiller. It never enhanced my life, only for short period of time when I was younger, when I lived with you.

It benefitted your second wife, though- the one who has nothing to do with me and the kids. She won't be walking anywhere that's for sure, probably taking cabs or driving a brand-new car. To be honest, she hardly eats, so buying food will not be a hardship for her. I think how life was when I did live with you, Catching black cabs everywhere. Never having to think if I have money, but I was working then, and I was on my own and free.

My life is so different from those days.

Daddy, if only you knew all the men that tried their luck with me, you would be shocked.

In the 70s and 80s most of the groups were very camp. I remember hearing you say that a lot of men had gay experiences to further their careers in the music business- some that were working in ATV music too. Is that why you told me you had done everything, talking about sexual experiences? I had often wondered what you meant by that.

Mummy always tells me that story when you took her to a party, and everyone had to put their keys into a large bowl. Some woman came up to you, and you were talking and smiling with her, When Mummy saw what was happening, she knew something wasn't right and told you that you had to go home now.

You see Daddy, you weren't so perfect, were you?

Those days were so exciting, but cannot replace the deep emotions and joy I feel today. I would rather be partying with my children. Your grandson, the one who occasionally saw you and listened to you intently when you spoke briefly to him, he went to school to pick up his GCSE exams. I know he is clever but as I told you Daddy, he took your death badly, plus he was grieving for his good friend too, from school. Every time I think of her, I get upset. I hope she is looking down on him and saying, "Well done Tyrone, you passed your exams."

You should be so proud of him, Daddy, and you should be very proud of me, too. I encouraged him to study hard, his head Teacher encouraged him, too. I kept saying how proud you would be of him. (This was a lie, but I just wanted to encourage my son to do well and study for his exams) He bloody well did it. He was with his friend when I called to find out if he had passed. Hhis friend heard me saying how proud I was of him and that I was crying. Tyrone told me that his friend cried too and said, "That is so lovely, your Mum loves you so much."

I am going out now to buy him food for his favourite meal. I put £10 aside. I am making him steak and chips with mushrooms his ultimate favourite meal followed by a dessert with ice cream. I know he likes vanilla cheesecake or apple pie. I phoned Mummy immediately to share the good news. She was so happy and proud of her grandson. She has to go to hospital for a check-up about her heart, so Tyrone will go there in the afternoon. Of course, I told his sisters who are very happy for him. Jade came around with a cake for him, and Mummy came around later. She came with her walking stick because she can hardly walk now, plus she is waiting for a hip replacement. It is so sad to see her like this Daddy, but she made the effort to come around and congratulate her grandson. She has always done her best to be a good mother, grandmother and great grandmother

Tyrone texted your lady to tell her that he had passed his exams. I don't know why he did this, maybe it was a knee jerk reaction, like when we called you to notify you about things that were going on in our life. You had no idea you never even called me up.

I remember the time I left your house and had an anaphylactic shock. My head had swollen to twice its size and by the time Max, Mummy's partner drove me to Accident and Emergency, my throat was closing up. I was whisked to the acute area and put on a heart machine. I remember so many doctors standing around me; they just appeared out of nowhere. As I was injected with something, I asked the nurse if I was going to die, I was so scared. I had something around my mouth too. "Hopefully not on my shift," She said.

I started praying to God because I knew it was life-threatening. After what seemed like an eternity, I was taken to a ward to recover. I remember Mummy and her partner Max coming, my daughter and her husband. When I told you about this, Daddy, you said to me, and I remembered those words I will never forget what you said to me, "Isn't that a good story?"

Did you think I would really lie about something like that, Daddy?

Even your Lady saying to me many years later, "It wasn't an anaphylactic shock." Really? Is that why I have to carry around an EpiPen? Who is she a Doctor?

Again, you dismissed what I said because it wasn't Important to you. I wasn't important to you. Of course, she knew everything. Well, she certainly knew how to extort money from you. You never complained about that to the family, did you? I remember going with a friend to see a show she told you to invest money into. I think you made a loss but that was okay because she was everything in your eyes, Daddy. I wondered why she suddenly became a little bit nice to me a few months before you died. Was that because she wanted you to think she would continue to have a relationship with us when you died? Haha. If only you knew Daddy.

You know for about 30 years, all I wanted was to hear you say for once in my life that you were proud of me.

That did eventually happen, near the end of your life, when I was in the newspaper for a painting I had done of Stormzy.

It was while doing arts and crafts with your great-grandson that I discovered I could paint.

What about the times I had written songs with my cousin who was a professional singer and songwriter? You never tried to help us. You were the only one that could be successful, how you craved the adulation of others. You were the only one that could be in the limelight. You and your lady, that was your world, and that was all that mattered.

The scars on my arm are still visible, faint but still there. It is the scars in my mind and heart that will never heal.

I am still that broken child. Cynics may say get over it already. Laying myself bare and writing the truth, getting it all off my chest has not only been therapeutic for me but made me realise I am not worthless. I have taken my responsibilities seriously and stepped up to the mark Daddy. As for all the cynics, well I have had a lot of that in my life, so really, Daddy, I should be used to that. People can say what the hell they want, but unless they have walked in my shoes and experienced what I have been through and tried for over 30 years to get back their father's love, they will never comprehend, never, ever. I am proud of your achievements in your life, but as a father, you didn't have a clue. I might not have the money you had, but if I did, I would help my children so much and give them my time too.

Daddy when you broke my heart in two, my world fell apart. I would behave disgracefully with men, if they never called me, I would call them up and demand to know why. You see, maybe they didn't like my body, my thick thighs, my stomach., Maybe they just wanted to have sex with me, and no strings attached. I wasn't attractive or slim enough. I would put myself through hell always overthinking and punishing myself, but now I think it is their loss.

You and your family always commented on my weight. Who gave you all the right to assassinate me and so I spent pointless years on ridiculous diets and pills? The diet pills gave me so much energy, and that feel-good factor. My low moods were pushed away, but the anxiety came back with a vengeance and reared its ugly head. If I wasn't contacted shortly by my dates after we parted the next day, I would lash out at them verbally and became an ugly aggressive, nasty female that argued with everyone. I would push them away because love doesn't stay, nothing is permanent and so to protect myself, I was always the one who ended it.

When true love comes, everything falls into place. Your heart beats for the other person. There is no waiting for their calls or texts. You think of them, and at that precise moment, they think of you too. You can take on the world, knowing they have given you the strength and happiness that completes your life. I've never had this love in my life.

You see Daddy you always told me men would be knocking on my door and I love the attention they give me and the power I have over them, but it is not love it is sex. I make no excuse for being a warm, hot-blooded, passionate heterosexual woman. You talked about me to everyone, didn't you? However, you were hardly Mr. squeaky clean. The habit of putting me down fed your ego and made you feel good, especially when you were hardly with a blushing virgin. People who live in glass houses shouldn't throw stones.

Whilst bringing up my children, I put my needs on the back burner and concentrated on bringing them up. Now they are all adults; it is my time to shine. You used to tell me that I had to stay with them in the night. I did that because you said so, you were God, and I wanted to please you so much, always looking for your approval, looking back it was rather pathetic. I find it so tragic that I listened to your every word and tried to live my life so you would be proud of me, but it was all in vain.

Do you know Daddy the pain and heartache I've felt all these years, once you met her, trying to regain your friendship and love? No daughter should have to feel the painful way I did, trying to get attention from their father. I wanted to hear nice things from you or you to give me attention, but instead, when we did speak, I had waited a whole month to tell you things, so I blurted everything out at once. Excuse me if I did become emotional. When there was something that really troubled me, I would phone you to tell you but nine out of ten times she would answer the phone and say your father was in a meeting or in the shower. I had no direct access to you.

You see Daddy, all my life you were that successful songwriter manager producer who was always busy, everyone wanted your attention, I was your daughter your flesh and blood, and yet I was at the bottom of your list. Internally I always knew this, but I could not accept it.

Now you are no longer here, Daddy. I feel I can be true to myself. I think I fully deserve as a grand-mother to find the time for myself. You al-ways used to lament when we saw you that life was short. Yes, it is, and I am living it now. I sometimes wonder if my newfound freedom comes in the form of a tablet but wherever it comes from it has enhanced my life. I am not mad; my brain just doesn't make serotonin, like others. A lot of the issues I have are from you.

However, I thank you for approving of my paintings but was it because of the mere fact the director who was filming the Stormzy video song bought my painting for him because Stormzy liked it. The director told me that it will be a memento of the filming. They filmed Stormzy singing his number one hit 'Blinded by your Grace' around the council flats next to The Hugh Corbett Centre in London, where my paintings were exhibited. I was called in on the Wednesday to sign the painting for Stormzy.

I was in a few newspapers because they were interested in my story that I discovered I could paint. At the time I was painting Grime artists, so I got the nick-name of Grime Gran. I was always artistic but concentrated on writing.

When you died Daddy, we all grieved in our own way and are still grieving. I am still on the tablets because of my depression, PTSD, and anxiety disorder all exacerbated by your death which I can't or rather don't want to go through. I am a strong woman, but the grief cuts my heart like a knife. Every nerve, every emotion is heightened. Bereavement makes us think about our own mortality: our past, present and future life. We don't realise that every day is a gift. The Lord giveth and the Lord taketh.

I remember feeling guilty for being me, as you seemed to sit in judgment over my life, especially when you and she were together in the earlier years. I listened hanging on to every word you said because you were Tony Hiller, the successful manager and songwriter. She was some ex-alcoholic you had met through your friend at The Health Spa. You gave her such creedence and a license to disrespect me. Suddenly after sharing our lives together, you started putting me down, when you met her, you abandoned me and your love and caring grew less over the years.

Daddy do you know how that felt? I missed you, and I missed our love and friendship. And then being talked about to family telling them all that I was mad and bad and promiscuous it broke my heart in two. It didn't have to be this way! Why was I suddenly the enemy? You had done this to Mummy too didn't you, when you walked out on her, in fact even your dealings with people in the music business were like this.

When you went off people, or they dared to disagree with you, you branded them mad. You would call say "mad cunts" that was one of your favourite sayings. Because of this and the huge physical and mental suffering, I was going through, I had suicidal thoughts and once was within a millimetre of severing a major artery. That is what the doctor told me. A lovely Northern Ireland Jewish man. Whenever Mummy took me, he would finish by saying to me, in his very thick accent, he wished me only to be well.

Well now you are no longer here I don't have to account for anything I do. I paint, I write, I create. I am trying to make money from my creativity for the children and me. I am not skinny. I am large-framed, and I have accepted myself for who I am. I am a beautiful person, Daddy, inside and out, and no one is ever going to make me feel bad about myself ever again.

I love you Daddy

RIP xxx

Letter 13

Dear Daddy,

I was up extremely early today, but too fatigued to jump in the shower and get dressed. I opened up my bedroom window, and the sun warmed my face. I inhaled on the cigarette, yes, I am still smoking. I can hear you telling me off.

I look at the flowers growing in the earth bed. The bright yellow and orange flowers planted haphazardly amongst the green plants which I think are weeds, but they look nice. A few bluebells are scattered everywhere. Some of the green plants with their thick leaves have grown onto the lawn making the edges crooked, but imperfections are attractive. The hedge that divides my gardens and the neighbours is an absurd shape because mummy's partner refuses to use an electric trimmer same as when he mows the lawn with a manual mower that makes a wonderful whooshing sound when he pushes it on the lawn, but all it does is flatten the grass. I have seen the very same mower displayed in a museum. He never asks to mow the grass he just does it, and I should imagine I would receive a small fortune from him if he paid for all the paddling pools and back door fences he had broken. Still, it is one less thing for me to do, and I should be grateful.

I moved into this house after my first child was born. I was young, and we had our life to look forward too. I remember when I first lived there with no central heating. Waking up in a very cold house, I would light the fire and the smell of sulphur lay pungent in the air. They were wonderful times but sometimes lonely. I would take the baby, my daughter everywhere with me in her straw cradle or the pram. I wouldn't leave her for a moment. The door in the front room is still not very good after all this time. Remember when you visited you were worried that the baby was not responding, and that she may be dead, so you called out her name and kept slamming the door shut? It's never been the same since.

Years later, as I breathe in the fresh morning air, I feel grateful that I have a roof over my head, but I never thought I would now be a single grandmother struggling. However, my house is a home, sometimes it is like Piccadilly circus here with all the family coming and going, but you know what Daddy? I love it, it's a normal family Home. I am now the proud mother of three children all grown up and a grandson. Daddy you never ever said to me how well I was bringing up the children. She never had any children and hated them, and she couldn't bear it if any one of the kids made a noise. But you and she had the relationship I wanted. You both had huge amounts of love for each other, so, why was she so vindictive toward me and take you away from me, when we were extremely close at one time.

It never had to be like this; we were a family once. She was just jealous of me and obviously felt threatened, and I can't think for the life of me why? She wanted you all to herself. She always said snide remarks to me or behind my back about me even my girls noticed it, but it was not a competition, Daddy, well at least not for me.

One of the first memories I have of you, Daddy, is warming my knitted white cardigan by the heater and burning it. Having piggyback rides and such fun times with you. I was always a Daddy's Girl, and you could do no wrong in my eyes. Oh my, how it all changed.

I remember an acquaintance of mine coming to my house for the first time and saying how rich I was. Really my house is in a terrible state. It needs a new modern bathroom, and I need carpet on the floor, but I had all my children close to me, even the animals follow me around. I have my art and my writing, so I guess I am rich Daddy, but not in the sense that you would think of riches.

My friend asked if I had room for a man in my life? After two failed marriages and kissing a lot of frogs in between I've never really given up hope of finding my prince, that would be the icing on the cake, the last piece of the jigsaw to complete my life. I want to meet my soul mate.

Has he come too late or is there such a thing as too late? The seasons come every year. The animals know at what precise time to mate, the trees and plants know when to form a bud which will form into leaves on the tree or flowers. There is a time for everything-the natural rhythm of life. We all have to wait until it is our time to receive the world's jewels.

Did you know Daddy that I love the evenings, the boys are upstairs, and the house is quiet? I relish lying across the settee. I am free to do as I wish, which is usually playing Candy Crush, frustratingly stuck on a level, or going into my art room/studio and working on a new painting. Of course, being with a very special person would add a different dimension to my evenings and life. That hope keeps me going. Why can't I have a happy ever after? I am hopeless at being loved, but I am a lioness when it comes to loving someone.

For years I have been the captain of the ship, but I don't feel that I reached my destination. Often, I feel like asking someone else to take over and jumping overboard.

You always promised to look after me, after all, you had the means. Now I am struggling more than I have ever done. I feel the pressure mounting against me.

I feel like my ship is sinking but I am too tired now to steer it anywhere. I shall hand over the wheel to my children. I can't worry about what will happen. I want to find my way back home. However, without money, one is a prisoner. Although I like to make the best of what I do, I have used every single penny of my money. I need a few more people to buy my art or a businessman like the one who bought a painting off Bradley Theodore for millions of dollars. I will probably start working in McDonald's for a minimum wage if I am lucky. Is this really what I have to look forward too.

If you truly loved us, Daddy, you would have changed your will to include us. Because of you going back on your word and lying to me, I actually hate you. It's not just about money Daddy, but at the end of the day, I'm a single parent who has raised three children and a grandson, and you knew how hard it was for me, and you had the ability to make my life so much easier. Once upon a time, you were my everything. We were friends and so close. You couldn't have truly loved me or my children to not want to help us in any way.

Because of you, Daddy I can't have a normal relationship. You leaving was the worst timing and fucked up my life big time. I was learning to walk and write again. My mind messed up from being in a coma, and the next year you just walked out. Why hadn't you or Mummy sought me professional help then it could have saved me from the suffering I have endured all my life. A year or two later you sent me to psychiatrists because you told the whole family I was crazy.

I wasn't crazy Daddy I had suffered a serious head injury, and I was just trying to deal with everything that had happened to me, the mental and physical scars will always remain with me, but I keep fighting. I am now tired of it. I don't want to continue fighting just to stay alive. Unless there is something brighter ahead, I will just curl up again on the settee, but this time not wake up.

A person can only take so much disappointment. It is a real struggle to live some days. I try so hard each day to inject some creativity into my day and get enthusiastic about everything.

Sometimes I feel death is the easier option. I won't have to worry about lack of money then.

You and she used to be out nearly every night in some posh restaurant in Mayfair or Knightsbridge the cost of your meal, for the two of you, just for one night Daddy, is more than I get to live on for a week to feed 4 of us and the pets. Never mind at least I know the value of money, and I have learnt how to budget. Only because I've had to, but when I have miscalculated or had to spend extra one week I know, worse way, I can ask Mummy, she might have a moan, but in the end, she helps me because she loves her grandchildren and me.

Love you, Daddy

RIP xxx

Letter 14

Dear Daddy,

Do you remember when we lived in the very big house in Hadley Wood? We were a real family then, being young I never really appreciated the lifestyle we led. The large driveway was terracotta tarmac which led on to steps that led to the Mahogany heavy wooden doors with white pillars either side. Beyond the drive the front garden was a continuation of Hadley Wood, only a road separated our house from the woods. I had walked in the woods so many times, especially with our neighbour, Olivia Newton-John and her two red setters called Geordie and Murphy. She lived with Bruce Welch of the hugely popular group The Shadows.

I was always popping next door into her house. Olivia Newton-John was an attractive, very slim lady and used to give me her clothes. I remember the dress with the bold yellow and black flowers and the knee-high suede boots that just about did up, even though I was young.

You know Daddy you and the whole of your family took away my self-confidence. You were always going on about weight. It seemed anyone who was thin was wonderful even if they were murderers. The first thing anyone would say is that I had gained weight-nothing to do with how I was feeling, what steps had I taken to help mankind. That just paled into insignificance, it was all about my weight, and that set my path to a life of starving then binging. Yes, I had a very unhealthy relationship with food, but now I like to nurture my body with my delicious food.

I like my cupboards to be bulging, and heaving stocked up with food. Heaven forbid there was a shortage of food. Food is love. Food is sexual. We use our mouth and tongue, sometimes fingers to lick and suck. Why should I not eat the good food I enjoy. Life seems to be all about pleasure being taken away from us. Even though you were all poor, your mother managed to feed a large family. She took such pride in her large dishes of food which were made with love, so you always told me. I know you missed her every day. You loved her so much. She was a very large lady. Was it only your Mother that could be big? Weight is a way of men controlling women.

My very small fridge is always full, although it is not large enough for the family. I am surprised I never had an eating disorder although there was a time that I was borderline. I saw food as the enemy. I couldn't eat like a normal person. I would be a typical yo-yo dieter, but the fact was that I was not huge. I am a strongly built woman. It is so pitiful that I spent absolute years hooked on diet pills, and my feeling of achievement and self-worth was tied to the bathroom scales. We are so much more.

All I can say Daddy is, "Thank goodness for the African culture who love real women." The more flesh one has, the more beautiful the woman. I see plus-size models and young women now who embrace themselves for who they are, and I absolutely love that. They wear figure-hugging clothes, and they own it, and men love the large breasts spilling over—big booties and thighs. As a woman I think there is nothing sexier than a woman with ample flesh yet when I stand naked in the mirror, I can still hear all the negative comments spoken, because I wasn't a perfect 10.

I should be proud of my stomach that gave birth to three large babies and not a stretch mark in sight. My stomach deserves respect and to be loved because it is part of me. I never had any problems in attracting the opposite sex, never. I remember once because you were always commenting on my size, I went to the doctor's and broke down and through sobs, I asked her, who has the right to comment on my weight? I felt I was judged purely on this and nothing else. I believe this ridiculous idea that all women should be a certain size was a way of controlling us. So many of my women friends wouldn't live their life because they wanted to lose weight first. They put their lives on hold until they reached a certain size.

Growing up we were not permitted to be different, all females had to resemble a Barbie doll, and if you were not blue-eyed and blonde haired you felt you were not attractive, it is almost parallel to Hitler's idea of creating an Arian race. This is a warped idea by fashion designers that all women should resemble adolescent boys. All I can say is thank goodness most of us have moved on, and London is now a diverse place. Beauty comes in all shapes and sizes love does not come in kilos age religion or colour. Funny thing is, which you seemed to deny, like everything else, you were the one, who at 15, introduced me to diet pills. Do you think that's right Daddy, putting your 15-year-old daughter on slimming pills just so my appearance could be pleasing to you?

Often, I would see Hank Marvin from The Shadows and Cliff Richard. Olivia Newton-John was a lovely woman and gave me a lot of time. I was always popping into her house. I remember the night surprisingly being on the red carpet with my then best friend at the premiere of Grease. I had no idea how big a deal this night was, and was certainly underdressed for it. We went to the after-party too. My life was certainly exciting when I was younger—a far cry from how it became.

Do you remember Daddy, our family home, down the slope on the right were three more houses? The Delmar's lived in the first house, and their front-drive was covered in pebbles. Norman Delmar was a conductor of The Royal Philharmonic Orchestra. He looked a bit like the Duke of Edinburgh. His wife Pauline was a most wonderful woman with an extremely posh accent. She had grey hair that framed the loveliest face. They had two sons. When they had heard of my car accident, Pauline told my Mother I could use their swimming pool anytime I liked. Their small swimming pool was just off their kitchen and was indoors.

When I look back, I think what wonderfully hospitable people they were. I used to just knock on their door any time, any day, they would open their home to me, a rare breed of people. They used to play croquet in their garden, the epitome of an upper class very lovely family. Their house was all white and looked different from the other large mock Georgian houses with the two huge pillars, either side of the doors. It was strangely called The Witching's. One of their sons' bedrooms (I think Robin) used to be facing the side entrance of the kitchen. I would stand there for ages as a young child looking across at the woods, probably much to his annoyance, as he used to sit facing out at the window. I can feel the coldness of the toilet and laundry room that was adjacent to the huge double garage which housed Mummy's cream coloured mini and your light blue Audi. The terracotta tiles added to the freezing cold of the rooms, but I found it fascinating being in those rooms; it was my hideaway.

As a child there was always somewhere to explore in our large house. Our house was built on a hill. The lawn in our back garden saw many a badminton tournament with your family—wonderful, happy family times. Remember the weeping willows that stood either side of the lawn? The back garden sloped off to a steep hill. There was even large steps going down to a path which led to a huge open room. I often wondered why it wasn't used as anything. My brother's room had a balcony that was never used by him. He had a hexagon-shaped toffee tin full to the brim with pennies that he had saved. I often went in his room and came out with a generous handful. Every morning on a school day the whole of the upstairs smelt of Brut aftershave and deodorant. Especially the bathroom we shared with its blue bath and toilet. I used to shut the door in the evening and have many a sneaky cigarette out of one of the windows. The spare bedroom was used to sleep the private nurse, that had to live with us after I came out of my coma and came home, she was there to look after me. The second private nurse you hired used to let me smoke her cigarettes.

At one point, your group The Brotherhood of Man used to rehearse in that room. I remember hiding behind the door watching them practice their dance routines and listening to their beautiful harmonies. A million times that house appears in my mind and dreams. I always imagine going through the double doors again and being ecstatic and pretending that Mummy kept the house. Mummy always said it was an unlucky house. She said the grounds belonged to the convent hundreds of years ago and a Nun committed suicide in the grounds. I haven't been able to substantiate her claim. It was there in Georgian House, Hadley common, that so much happened, good and bad times but the scared, confused girl who I became when you left. It has never left me to this day, and the harrowing attempts I went to, just so I could see, you are part of the house´s spiritual history.

I used to love walking and exploring the woods, which was far beyond our driveway. I remember the long grass and a tree that I used to climb with my best friend. Do you remember that tree, Daddy?

On a Sunday, I would take the dog for a walk. In fact, I would take him to The Hadley Road Pub, which was only 5 minutes away. I used to meet friends in there and felt very left out as they were going home to their Sunday Roast dinner, this was more of a British/ Christian tradition. On Sundays, we ate our bagels in the morning, and our meal was Viennas and chips or egg and Vorsht/salami. I wanted our family to eat roast dinners like everyone else.

I always insisted that we had a Christmas tree to stand in our huge lounge, and longed to decorate it with you Daddy, like they do in all the Christmas movies. But sadly, Daddy, you were never around to do it. You were always in recording studios or travelling abroad with the Brotherhood of Man. I didn't want to feel different from my friends. Because you were in the music business, religion never dominated our lives; assimilation not segregation.

I used to spend lots of time walking the dog in Hadley Woods, that was until one day after school. I was half way in the woods, near the railway line that ran from Hadley Wood Station. As I walked Major, our little Yorkshire Terrier on the lead, to the left of me was a man with his trousers down to his ankles-his hand seemed to be moving along his exposed penis. I had never seen anything like this in my life. Frightened, I turned around to get back on the main pathway. He chased after me. I let go of the dog as I jumped down from the trees with their roots to the main path. Stumping my stomach in the fall on one of the branches, I carried on running and holding my stomach. I remember getting to the bit where people parked their cars. A man asked if I needed help, but I worried he might be an accomplice, so kept on running. The hill I was running up seemed to last forever, but I managed to get home safe, and we reported the incident to the police. Major had followed me home with his brown leather lead trailing on the floor.

How many times had I dreamt Mummy still owned the house? My tears and blood are deep within the walls. I am sure that if I came back as a ghost, I would haunt that house. I had gone through so much when I lived there and experienced you walking out on us, which set the precedence for any relationship. No man was able to make me feel secure. I realised that my taste in men was abominable. The ones who were the good guys I wasn't interested in because I was used to a lot of drama and after all, if there was a happy ever after, there is no drama. I thought love was always painful because that is what I had experienced as a young teenager.

I remember when we were kids, every week you bought a huge brown bag stuffed with chocolates for my brother and me I can see you now kneeling down next to the very polished sideboard which everyone seemed to have in their dining room in those days. As a young child, you would read bedtime stories to me and make funny sounds for the characters. You had a way of bringing the book to life, and my love for reading grew that is why from babies I got my children into books. From the first plastic books you put in the bath, to books you put on the handles of the buggy to picture books and beyond.

Some Sundays you would take us out to a restaurant often with your father, Sam. I always remember him with his grey mac over his suit, shirt and tie. He was a smart man. A folded-up newspaper would be in his pocket, thick black-rimmed glasses covered up his smiling face. He always wore a checked cap and out the side of his mouth a cigar would constantly dangle.

I loved to hear the love story of how Sam Hiller as a young man who lived in America with his family, worked for his uncle Joe Hiller in the music business. You told me he was a very talented man, and had worked with the Marx brothers. Sam was assigned to go to England and pick up some sheet music. The only way to travel then was by boat. Whilst on the boat he got friendly with a man called Barney Schreiber. When the ship docked in England Barney got Sam to promise he will come for a meal at his Mother's house. True to his word a week later, Sam turned up to see his new friend Barney. It was not just the beginning of a lifelong friendship; it was also the beginning of his new life. Unbeknown to Sam, Barney had a beautiful sister called Sarah. Her long, black, thick, wavy hair covered one side of her face as she was self-conscious about her mole. She was a voluptuous young woman. Her origins were Spanish/Portuguese. Sam took one look at this young woman of sixteen and fell madly in love. He never went back to America. He and Sarah got married in the Spanish-Portuguese synagogue in the East End of London. Unfortunately, it got destroyed in the war.

You always told me that Sam and Sarah lived in the East End of London that was ghetto to the Jewish population. They lived in Cookham Place. The family always called it Cookham buildings in Bethnal Green although it is near Arnold Circus in Shoreditch.

I went with my cousin Eric last year, who took me around where the Hiller family grew up. The flats with their red-bricked exterior overlooking the Bandstand was where you grew up. It is an oasis of calm and an attractive place. I never imagined this place to be so picturesque. I often meet up with Eric in Pellicis a family-run Italian business that was frequented daily by the Kray twins and all the gangsters of the time-a bygone era. The restaurant's walls, which are covered in wood, have not changed, nor has their home-made Italian food.

It is a listed building-a small cafe in Bethnal Green Road that is so popular that it has queues of people waiting for a table. The atmosphere is lively, and laughter fills the air and after I like to walk around Bethnal Green and up to Shoreditch, Whitechapel and ending up catching the train home in the manic Liverpool Street. It has the most eclectic mix of architecture mixed with state-of-the-art high buildings. Shoreditch is a vibrant, diverse place that makes London the great city it is. It is like going back in time, and I feel close to you, Daddy. Eric showed me where you lived and went to school. The bandstand was mentioned by you so many times. It was an absolute oasis of calm. I hadn't imagined you lived in such a wonderful place, but you never really told me in descriptive terms, so it was good to see it for myself.

After all the stories you told me about the East End and your Jewish hjistory I was so intrigued I went to the library and read up about it. I found out, Daddy, that the East End of London was home to Jewish immigrants from Poland, Russia, Ukraine, Romania, Germany, etc. Of course originally, they were not European Jews, but Jewish people originally classed as ethnoreligious and are Israelites/Hebrews. However, because of persecution, Jewish people became Nomads and lived in many different Countries, finally putting down their roots in Eastern Europe.

I remember hearing stories from you or your sister Eva of your life as a child. You had eight surviving siblings, and you all slept in one bed—the girls on one end and the boys on the other. Once a week, you all had a bath at the local swimming pool. The girls would stay up at night and sew clothes which were sold in a market stall the next day. Your Mother was a strong woman and kept the family together. It must have been so tough when Sam left her for quite some time. Every morning I heard she was up at 6 a.m. washing down the front step to her flat that was on the ground floor and cooking huge delicious trays of food. The only memory I have of her is sitting at the table as a very young child and Nanny Hiller passing a huge silver tray of chopped liver over my head. I heard how infamous your mothers' biscuits called Keir Charles were. You and your brothers' friends used to be handed some by Sarah Hiller through the kitchen window. I could not believe last year. I was standing in front of her window, the legendary Nanny Hiller. As I stood in front of the kitchen window, I could imagine her singing as she cooked huge quantities of food.

The family evenings were filled with singing, dancing and playing spoons. A happy, fulfilled life always seems to be measured by money, but it is a loving family that enriches your life. You always mentioned your childhood as idyllic times, even though they must have been tough. Coming from such a loving family, I wonder how you became a once a month father, grandfather and great grandfather. Your first love was show business, your siblings and then her. It used to also be me at one time. I know at 12 you were digging up dead bodies from the wreckage of the war. You apparently got a certificate for that. You and your brothers did whatever you could to stay alive in the overcrowded ghetto of the East End.

When I lived with you in Westbourne Terrace Mews, you always had a painting of Cable Street on the wall. Cable Street became the most popular anti-fascist victory to have taken place. The Jewish population and friends of the Jewish people blocked the road so the fascists could not march. Today the Jewish immigrants have been replaced by Muslim Asian immigrants. How I long to have one of those paintings or something to remember you by. Daddy, it is not fair that she has kept everything. She had nothing to do with your life with us. She has taken every single memory and memento. It is like you never existed- what a cruel, heartless thing to do. She is making us all suffer because the truth is, she was jealous. She controlled every aspect of your life, I always thought that DNA would always win, but sadly that isn't the case, but you know that Daddy, don't you? Just want you to know, Daddy, that I have asked her for a few things which were part of you for my children, your grandchildren, via my brother.

Unfortunately, she has not responded to my requests. I am your biological daughter, same as your grandchildren and great-grandson and we will not forget her callous, cruel attitude to us. The time will come when we will not be silenced anymore. I hope you are looking down from above and can see what is going on. However, whilst I am surrounded by my family, animals and friends, filling my days writing and painting amongst the motherly duties, I wonder if all the properties worth millions of pounds have made her happy at the expense of not having my children in her life or me? Well, Daddy, maybe its wishful thinking on my part, we weren't in your life before why would she want us in her life now.

I hope you have been looking down and seen what has been going on—the way the children and I have been treated. Five people came up to me at your Shiva/wake and asked who I was? They didn't even know you had a daughter let alone grandchildren or a great-grandson. Did you see the way we were all treated like strangers and not your family?

I was used to this, but do you understand the damage it had done to me? I felt downtrodden and everyone in the family ignoring me. I don't understand that when you married a second time, I was completely abandoned. You were my father, Tony Hiller the one I put up on a pedestal. I realise now that I loved Tony Hiller, the songwriter. To see you only once a month or every 6 weeks broke my heart. I was excluded when you had our American cousins over, she invited all the immediate family to the flat, but not me and my children. I only got in touch with them by chance on Facebook years later. They were perplexed as to why the children and I were not there that evening at your home. They too never knew I existed, but they do now.

I felt like the downtrodden daughter—the one you used to moan about because you just wanted your second wife. You should be very proud of your grand-children and grandson the ones you hardly saw. We shall carry on as before and pray that through our hard work and pulling together as a family. There is a bright future for us all.

As I told you on your death bed, I loved you so much. You are probably the only man I ever loved and looked up to. I have never been able to have a successful relationship. I blame you for that! I meet a man, but I know that it is not going to last from the beginning because my first and biggest love from you had been cruelly snatched away.

Firstly, after my accident, when I was restrained in the hospital, in a coma and nearly died, you walked out.

I had to do dramatic things for you to come and see me. Love hurts, and I can't handle it. Love is elusive to me. You set the precedence Daddy. Do you not realise how much you wounded me? I wonder how Mummy coped with you walking out after 20 years. She still speaks about that time, and I can see the tears well up in her eyes when she speaks about you, but she tries not to show emotion. I don't know how she carried on.

All my life, I searched for that wonderful love. When I look at my children and grandson, I am filled with pride. I got it right.

She told me in no uncertain terms that she didn't want me around. You didn't want me around either Daddy. There is a large part of me that has been rejected by you. This rejection will stay with me forever. You allowed her to be this way, to speak to me like this, you gave her the power to talk down to me. You let her rule the roost. I was never shown respect by any of you. Are these the days of equality?

A woman on her own is treated differently, which is why I have had to be that more assertive.

I remember when I called you up from Israel, Daddy, saying that I was returning to England. I thought you would be happy to see me. You told me that I couldn't come back to the house. But that was my bedroom! That was my home. The place I used to live. The restaurants we used to go to together. The wine bar I used to frequent regularly because I didn't like staying in the house alone while you were away touring all the time with the Brotherhood of Man. I was friendly with the late Milton Reid, the actor in one of the James Bond films. He was in that advert for

Condor. He was quite a character. Because he was a large man, he always wore culotte type trousers and cowboy boots. In one of his boots, he put his address book. We had good times there, and I remember driving in his huge American car and going to places with him.

You told me that she had turned my bedroom into a study for you and her. What about the clothes I left-really expensive ones, even that expensive Hermes scarf and all my perfumes? I didn't take them with and thought they would be safe in your house. You told me that she was living with you permanently and there was no room for me.

I couldn't believe what you were telling me. "Why can't we all live together?" I asked. "She got rid of the bed" you replied. I was in disbelief. But why I kept asking. Where am I meant to go? We lived there together, and when you were at home which wasn't very often, we would go out to showbiz parties, you were more like my friend. Suddenly she moved in, and every trace of me was gone. Even the clay figures I had made to decorate the lounge had gone.

I told you that Mummy had sold the house in Hadley Common and was living with her parents in Chiswick until she could move into her new house. "Phone your mother up and tell her you are coming back."

"What if there is no room?" I asked. I really wanted to see you and was very upset. How could you do this to me I kept thinking to myself, but I couldn't say this to you. Whatever you said was the rules. Maybe I didn't want a confrontation or maybe in hindsight when I look back at things, I should have grown some balls as the saying goes but as usual, I just accepted it. "There is no room for you here, She lives with me now, and there is no room for you."

In true form Mummy and my grandparents welcomed me with open arms even though before I went away, she was very hurt that you wanted me to testify against her in court, branding her mad so you wouldn't have to pay her maintenance. I wasn't called to court, but Mummy said that she would forgive me but not forget. I was so in awe of you, put you right up on a pedestal, but you used me as your weapon.

So, Daddy, you found a new woman and didn't want me to be around.

I remember going to your mews house after that and going up the familiar winding staircase to what was once my bedroom. I looked in a wardrobe that had her things in. Where had she put my stuff? No explanation why she had got rid of everything. The thing I can never forget is that there was no apology for getting rid of my stuff. You and she never gave me the respect to ask me if it was okay. You just got rid of every trace of me. You didn't want me to exist. Daddy, you walked out on us once when I desperately needed you, and now you wanted to be out of my life again... How could I ever forgive you?

Love you, Daddy

RIP xxx

Letter 15

Dear Daddy,

Time is a great healer. My memories of you are bitter-sweet. Tony Hiller the successful songwriter/record producer. You have left a great legacy of songs. You will always be best known for co-writing and producing, 'Save your Kisses for Me' by The Brotherhood of Man which is still the biggest selling Eurovision Contest winning song ever. They were the first group to choreograph a dance routine which set a precedence for the wonderful show the Eurovision Song Contest is today.

My favourite song of yours, though, is 'United We Stand' by the original Brotherhood of Man. I had no idea this song was recorded by over 100 artists, including Elton John. It was used so many times and made you millions. It must have been your favourite song as you requested it to be played in the crematorium. In the chapel, the wooden coffin was on display in front of where the congregation sat. Of course, there was just a brief mention that I was your daughter, and then it was all about you and her. Apparently meeting and marrying her were the best days of your life. Since you met her, it has been the demise of our relationship.

I wasn't able to convey my inner thoughts and feelings towards you because money dictated your time and your time dictated your life of which I was deprived of any with you.

When you died, I fell apart. I loved you so much Daddy, and you broke my heart by casting me aside. How I wish you were sitting at the table now, just you and me like it used to be, like it was when you cared about me. How I longed for me and you to be alone for 30 odd years, but you never gave me your time. Do you have any idea how that made me feel? You were not my Daddy then. I just called you 'My Father.' The successful songwriter / producer.

It was so important for you to be loved by people in the Music business and strangers, but I was your flesh and blood. Of course, it wasn't always like that. We used to go out socially together, show business parties, bars, restaurants, to your friends' houses, but that all ended abruptly.

What kind of man were you that none of us could just turn up at your door and see you?

My daughters have a front door key to my house and come and go as they please. I didn't want a key to your home, but I would have liked to have been able to pop in sometimes, especially if I was in the area and not just by appointment, same goes for your grandchildren.

I remember one incident when Jade went to walk the dog in Hyde Park. Later that afternoon she phoned me up really upset that the dog had dragged her through some mud. Her Jean's were wet and covered in mud. I told her to go to your house as you lived ten minutes away. She pressed the buttons, and surprisingly you answered the door. Jade told me later that you were okay about it, however she was not very happy, and when Jade asked if she could borrow a pair of your tracksuit bottoms, she looked Jade up and down and didn't think she had any to fit her insinuating that Jade was fat.

Jade had actually lost six and a half stone due to going for extremely long walks with the dog. When someone has struggled with their weight, they are extremely sensitive about it. She was thin through dieting. Surely, she knows how it is to struggle with your weight. After all she was rather plump when she met you. When Jade was leaving, she just put the muddy, wet jeans in a bag. She didn't even offer to have given them a light wash in the washing machine and put them in her drier.

Many times, when I was in Marble Arch, I so wanted to call you up Daddy and meet up for a coffee and a chat, but that normal occurrence was denied to me. 9 out of 10 times she answered the phone. She made it so hard for me to contact you. Even when I wanted to see you, there was always some excuse, and that feeling of being estranged by you only added to my sadness. That feeling of abandonment that I felt every day. Does wanting to be with a parent simply vanish when one is older?

I want to ask you that since you have departed this world, have you witnessed all that has gone on in my home and yours? Are you sorry for the comments you made about me? Every night I am home guarding my children, and home and not one man has been to my house. However, I shouldn't have to be justifying this to you now, after all your Dead. You used to tell the family I was a nympho, yes Daddy that's what you called me, because I used to go out dancing to the Empire Ballroom Leicester Square to listen to my cousin who sang with the Ray McVay Band. With my Peppermint cordial in one hand and my handbag in the other, all I wanted to do was dance the night away, however, because of the lies and the reputation you falsely gave me, plus when your famous friend seduced me when I was a teenager, you told the family all that I was promiscuous. Do you still think I'm mad and a nymphomaniac? That is what they all thought and still think. You even made up a song about me to get laughs at my expense.

You told everyone you gave me lots of money. You used to take the piss out of me and comment about me to the whole family. Do you think that was right or a decent thing to do? You slurred my character to the family. So, I need to ask you again, Daddy, why did you do that? Why did you slur my character? Why why why? Is it normal for a parent to lie about their child so their family could feel sorry for you? Like you were under so much pressure. Did I really cause you that much pressure? Because if I did, give me a sign now please Daddy, let me know your there, let me know you can hear me.

You never helped or encouraged me like other Daddies did for their children because you wanted to be the star—the centre of attention. You were an egomaniac.

It was all the terrible things you had said about me in the past that stuck with the family. The false and incorrect picture you built up of me has stuck in your brothers' and sisters' mind, but like me, they too are guilty of putting you up on a pedestal.

She really did keep us at arm's length with only a monthly visit which had to be booked into your diary which she kept for you. I once phoned you, Dad, as I really needed to speak to you and as usual she answered the phone. Upon requesting to speak to you, she told me you were out at a meeting, as it was really urgent I noticed in my contact list. I had your mobile number, so I phoned your mobile and she answered it. Ha, ha-ha so you weren't in a meeting was you? It was just another lie from her to keep me away from you.

Despite how cruel and unfair you were to me, I loved you so much and you not spending time with me gave me a lot of issues that I still have to work on. I want you to know how much I loved you even though you were never a proper Father to me.

I love you, Daddy

RIP xxx

Letter 16

Dear Daddy,

The experiences we have as a child definitely shape our lives and make us the people we are today. Our past, present and future are not separate; they are a continuation of our journey.

I hope from time to time you look down and see what is going on in our world. Amber came into the house yesterday very upset; she was really sobbing, so unlike her. Its times like this I would call you up always in a drama. Is that because I associate tears and drama with you, or because of the past when I was forever pleading with you to come and see me which you never did.

"Don't you know I will always love you?"

Those were the last words you ever spoke to me, was when you had a roomful of people visiting you, even as you were dying, I had to have a time slot when I could to see you. Eric told you that he played the Al Martino record on his radio show the previous Sunday, "Daddy loves you, Honey." The song you wrote for me. I moved to the top of the bed and said," I forgot you wrote that for me". You replied, " Sure." Your eyes were actually looking my way.

Finally with you making eye contact with me for the first time, I said, "I felt that you didn't love me anymore Daddy." I so wanted to tell you many more things in that fleeting moment, but that's all it was, a fleeting moment, not enough time then, that's why I'm writing to you now.

I so wanted to be alone with you, to speak with you, but I was denied that for absolute years.

Would it have hurt for us to meet for lunch or a coffee like we used to do? Once or twice a month? Why couldn't we have had some father/Daughter time?

Why did she always have to be with you spewing her nasty comments? I know she controlled everything about everything.

Once on my daily visits to the Princess Grace Hospital, in my allotted time, where you always had procedures, because of blocked stents, she wanted to leave you for a while, she had to go out of the hospital to do something, don't know what? She never really spoke to me enough to explain why she needed to leave, but you did not want that.

I tried and explained to you that I would be here with you and would not leave your side and assured you I would look after you. But you went crazy, you didn't want me there, you wanted her.

You lay on your Death bed; your now thin frame was covered in a freshly ironed pink shirt. Your voice was very quiet, but considering the circumstances, you were in good spirits. Always the entertainer right up until the end, you were on top form smiling at your showbiz friends but occasionally crying because this was to be your last performance. The next time I visited with Amber, you were sedated. She sobbed because your great-grandson had drawn you a picture and she was so sad that you would never see it. If you had, you wouldn't have wanted it, just like you never wanted his school photo, she would probably have had to take it home with her.

You said you loved Amber so much. The other grandchildren felt it. I remember you telling her many times, even as you were in your wheelchair being wheeled down to the operating theatre for one of your numerous procedures, that you would always look after her. In fact, you would always look after us.

Things that happen in the past, especially traumas, have a profound effect on our lives

The time after my accident, which still affects me, and then you walked out and I slashed my wrists, pleading down the phone and crying for you to come and see me. This did not make you come.

It proved to me that you were the only one that mattered to you. Do you know how that made me feel, especially as I was still recovering from the accident physically and mentally? I have always nursed a broken heart, but this was normal after all; you were Tony Hiller, the songwriter ex tough East End boy.

I used to be annoyed with Mummy's partner. Well he did interfere a bit too much, but he was and still is always there for my children. In fact, when you died, they actually said Mummy's partner Max was the real grandfather to them. You were just someone they saw once in a while, on their monthly booked in, strained appointment. But, for some reason, they still loved you. You were their Pappy. They loved your jokes you made them laugh. I am having a bad time realising that you were not the man I thought you were, yet I put you on a pedestal and idolised you. I wouldn't let anyone say a bad word about you.

It wasn't a normal scenario not to be able to see my father because she didn't want to be inconvenienced by the children and me, yet she would talk to other people about them just to make herself look good like she was the doting step-grandmother, but she never really knew them; I mean a few hours every 4 to 6 weeks does not really give you enough time to actually know someone. My children were never babysat or able to go to your house, let alone spend the night. Isn't that what grandparents do?

I tried to always be polite and respectful to her, making small talk, conversation, with her on numerous times, when we had our once a month visit. I tried so hard for your sake Daddy, but she would completely blank me when I spoke. She would make a stupid face to my daughters like taking the piss out of me, to them, behind my back; what did she think?

My daughters were not going to tell me what she was doing, or was she trying to get my daughters on her side too, so they could all rip my heart out and pull my limbs off one by one? Why did she hate me so much?

She was allowed to be as nasty as she wanted, to me, because you let her Daddy, you never stood up for me, your daughter, instead you backed her up, what was it, what did she have on you? Because I don't really want to believe that my Daddy the East End Boxer/ Street Fighter was really that weak.

Daddy, you allowed her to become The Boss and so began the demise of our relationship although now I realise that we never had a normal father/daughter relationship ever, only the one I made up in my mind.

I remember around six or seven years ago when you had a stroke. She would not let me see you. Every day I called her and pleaded with her to let me visit you as I needed to see you, in case you died, but she always made an excuse, like you were going to be moved to another hospital, or another room or you were waiting for the doctor to come, so many excuses just to keep me away from you. I just wanted to see you and I couldn't.

She made me feel like a nuisance, an outsider, but I was your daughter, and I just wanted to see for myself that you were ok. This woman, the woman you thought was a Goddess, who told me, as you lay on your bed, hours from death that she had bought another flat at the front of the building, she couldn't wait to tell me, that flat was hers too. I remember her proudly hitting her chest and her Cheshire grin, saying, "It's mine all mine."

That was the last time I was to see you, Daddy. I sat with you saying Hebrew prayers. All the time the door was wide open, how I longed for it to be shut so there was just you and I, but this was never to be. Before I left the room, I went up and caressed your face something I would never dare do when you were alive. You would have pushed me away and told me I was mad.

I looked down as you lay sedated, hours from death. I told you that I loved you so much but could never forgive you for the way you had treated us all, for the way you let her be rude to me, I told you how much your absence from my life caused so much unhappiness. The years I lived knowing I was not important to you. My girls were telling me that you told them you only bother with me because you felt sorry for me, because I was in that horrific accident—what a heartless thing for a father to say.

As a parent that is not something a normal parent remarks on or even comments about especially to my children, but you were so good at that. You were filling my head as a young child calling Mummy mad and bad. Calling all the younger cousins cunts, and you, dear Daddy walking out on your family when they needed you the most, so tell me, who's the cunt now? Was it too much for you? Obviously, you couldn't handle it and took the cowards way out. You walked out. Was it because having a Family interfered with your beloved music business life? That was your priority.

After I sat with you, I went back into the lounge. Her friends were sitting on the sofa. One of them had bought a load of sandwiches and crisps, that particular friend of hers was the one that sat by your death bed stroking your hand and thanking you for all the holidays you sent her and her children on and paid for them, too.

I tried to join in the conversation, her friends were conversing with me, but she didn't, she was cold and distant. I noticed how dark and gloomy the flat looked. The only sunshine was in the bedroom where you lay. I cannot put into words what it feels like to live in the shadows, when my teenage years were full of showbusiness glitz.

I had to carry this feeling of disregard and rejection most of my life. Is it any wonder I had to deal with self-confidence issues and still do to this day?

So, Daddy, I want to talk to you about your 80th birthday party, which she had arranged, she had done the table plans the menu the everything. It was in a London hotel, it was exactly there when I realised, I was nothing in your life.

You remember Daddy, you were sitting with her on the top table with your brothers and sisters. I thought we should be sitting there with you, or at least the next table. Instead, the children and I were put on a table, right at the back of the hall, away from everyone. I remember it was the closest table to the toilets. The table was away from the others, completely isolated, but then she had arranged your party so what should have I expected?

When you made your speech you never even mentioned us or the fact that you even had children and grandchildren; it was bad enough we were sitting the furthest away from you, but not even a mention of us in your speech. I think that was absolutely disgusting and extremely hurtful. Since that evening, I have had to accept the fact that we meant absolutely nothing to you!

I remember after I left you, for the very last time, I went to Paddington station and sat on a bench in the smoking area. I listened to my cousin Eric Hall's radio show, but the reception was bad.

When I returned home later, I was cooking a saucepan of spaghetti, and she called.

I remember concentrating on the spaghetti standing upright in the large cooking pan being softened and cooking in the boiling water. I let the mobile ring and Amber told me to pick it up.' It's her, "I said. She never normally calls so Amber and I looked at each other and knew it had to be bad news.

Amber phoned her back. She said, and these were her exact words. "Tony had died" not even your Grandfather, your Pappy, my father. Amber asked her what time you had died, and she said at 8.15, very precisely.

Daddy, I could not cry for that moment, Amber was distraught, and I hugged her close.

Nobody tells you or talks about bereavement in this country. Maybe it is because we are all petrified of not existing anymore. People deal with their grief differently. Amber left her boyfriend and threw herself into work; she just worked all the time. That was her way of dealing with it.

After I had heard that you had died, I had a delayed shock, as later kneeling down in front of the bedside cabinet, I lit a candle and said prayers for you- my Daddy the big, strong man, my Daddy, the hero. I remember when I brought Eric to see you.

You were work colleagues, best friends and uncle and nephew. He hadn't seen you for a couple of years. I remember telling him that you didn't have long and whatever happened between the two of you to forget about it.

She had made sure Eric hardly came to see you, too. In the end, she won Daddy. You both lived in a bubble, and she got you to rely on her more and more, in fact, she used to control your everything. I was so overcome with grief that the T-shirt I was wearing I ripped open revealing my bra.

At that point, my dear friend and neighbour came to pay her respects. I ran down the stairs, not thinking and opened the door. I must have looked a sight, but at that precise moment, I didn't care.

I waited all my life to hear you say you were proud of me and you did once about a year before you died. You were proud of me because of my paintings, because I was in the newspaper. She actually said she loved my paintings, which was probably why you said you loved them too. If she hadn't liked them, then maybe it would have been a different story.

I remember when you were in the hospital, nobody thought you would make it, from my phone I showed you a photo of your portrait which I had painted. You laughed at it, when you saw it, but your dementia was bad, so I didn't take it to heart. But why did you laugh Daddy?

Like the time I saw you on your 91st birthday, I bought you a birthday cake with gold paper plates and napkins. You were able to sit on a chair then. You kept telling me and your grandkids how tired you were and weren't very sociable with us, but as soon as a neighbour walked in and had come to see you, you started talking a smile appeared on your face, and you seemed really happy. The candle on the cake played happy birthday continuously. My girls told me to turn it off, but you said you liked it.

So, we let it play continuously. How dreadfully sad that my children and I saw you more than we had ever seen you in years when you were ill and dying. After all, I was only your daughter, the one you wished you never had, once you met her.

You may have written the worldwide hit that won The Eurovision Song contest, 'Save your Kisses for me.' But there was and will be, **'No more Kisses for me.'**

Love you, Daddy

RIP xxx

Letter 17

Dear Daddy,

I went out with my grandson today. He has missed me terribly as Mummy took him and Amber away to the seaside for a few days, which was such a lovely gesture as Amber should have been away with her now ex-boyfriend.

Mummy felt sorry for her and wanted to cheer her up. What a wonderful gesture. You see, that is what families do. They sent me video clips every night of them all and Mummy and her partner of over 30 odd years sitting together enjoying the evening's entertainment in the hotel. My kids will always have such fond memories to look back on of Mummy and Max. They have made memories together.

You never took your grandchildren on holiday, even though you and she were always taking holidays in Spain. You never even took your Grandchildren on a weekend break nor a day out to the coast.

Mummy is old now. Her body is in pain from her various ailments, and she can hardly walk and yet she still involves her grandchildren and great-grandson in her life.

One thing I will never have is that special Mother and daughter relationship because of you.

Daddy, I am sobbing now. You brainwashed me against Mummy. My attitude towards her was learned behaviour. You were the one, since I was a child, that told me Mummy was mad, you poisoned me against her. I remember that whenever we had time together, you would go on about her all the time. I even remember you speaking badly to one of Mummy's cousins about her and that just confirmed in my childlike mind that everyone knew she was mad and bad. You were the parent that even when I was young, I didn't see that much but you were adored by everyone, and you were worshipped by me.

Mummy really needs to live in a bungalow. She has paid to install a chairlift in her house because she struggles with the stairs; she can't walk up them any more. She and Max were discussing moving to another area, but they decided against it because they wanted to stay to be near me and see that I was okay. I never embraced that. They have always been there for me, unlike you. How absolutely despicable that you did this, you robbed me pure and simple.

Mummy told me she first set eyes on you in Leicester Square. Apparently, you were taking photos of people, mainly tourists. You would take down their name and address and their payment upfront, but you never had any film in the camera. Did you really do this Daddy? Tut-tut. Like her, you made yourself an angel, but in actual fact doing this to innocent tourists shows the other side to your character.

I feel so sorry for Mummy. She was only 17 when she met you—engaged at 18. Mummy told me how mean you were as a husband. She told me that she wanted to tile the kitchen, but you wouldn't give her the money for the tiles she wanted, and so she bought the ones that were going cheap. They were really for swimming pools as that was all she could afford with the money you gave her. I wondered why our kitchen was so blue. Seriously Daddy.

Now, I look at Mummy, and I think she was so brave. You lived rent-free in the maisonette in Chiswick that was owned by Mummy's parents, which is where we all first lived. Mummy's family really helped you, but instead of being grateful, you always told me what a horrible man her father was. Well, I don't think much of your taste. Look who you remarried some heartless woman who despised us and turned you against us. I hope you know the damage you have done to me the children and Mummy. She owns everything of yours lock, stock and barrel.

What did you do for your grandchildren, Daddy? A small window of your time? To give your time to someone is the most precious gift because time is all we can give to someone. We were just fitted in.

When we did spend a couple of hours in your company, you would always go into one of your big long speeches and talk about yourself and then tell your grandchildren how to live their live's.

You never asked them questions that showed any real interest in them, I remember you asking my eldest daughter hows school? Daddy, she was at University. Was that because you had a bit of Alzheimer's then? I know you always had sticky notes put on your computer with instructions on how to use it. You had those yellow sticky notes on there for years.

Amber was at work today and is out with friends, and Harvey is staying with his Daddy and wife for Eid. Such a wonderful contrast to me sitting here with the Shabbat candles flickering. You see there can be peace and love if you want. Your songs were always about peace and love. Especially the songs you wrote for the original Brotherhood of Man. Your favourite 'United we Stand.' 'Where are You Going to My Love.' 'Reach out Your Hand,' and others.

You used to sit there at your large dining room table and comment on us like we were a dysfunctional family when in fact we are a very harmonious loving family, and I am so proud of them all and proud of myself.

It's such a shame Daddy that you never once told me I was doing a good job, but you were just too busy with your own life and her and in your element with all your showbusiness friends. Nothing or no one else mattered.

After a year of asking and having to go through my brother, I eventually got the gold discs but not the ones I wanted. She owned everything. You never left me a thing!

I had them displayed on my wall, but when my girls saw them, they told me to take them down. Everything that has happened with her ignoring the family and us, they too now know who you really were, and they understand what I have been through. When I look at the Gold discs, now It reminds me of all those years ago when I was involved with The Brotherhood of Man. They were a huge part of my life.

Sometimes I would go with you into the recording studios and see them record. They were all so lovely towards me. I remember them all rehearsing at the house in Hadley common. I must have been the first person to see them perform the famous dance to the song, 'Save your Kisses for Me.'

I remember the gold chain and razor blade necklace that Martin and Sandra from The Brotherhood of man bought you on your birthday. They inscribed it, To our Bubala. I would have loved to have got that. Instead, I got sweet FA.

Daddy, I want to ask you, do you think you did enough? Did enough for me and the kids? You never left anything to anyone of them. It didn't have to be something of monetary value I'm talking about just something sentimental. Something that showed you existed.

At this present time, the Eurovision song contest fever is sweeping across the globe. There are so many countries involved now that there are different stages to see which countries will make the final. The performances each country gives are bigger and camper every year, absolutely wonderful. It is a spectacular programme. People all over the country are holding parties. Tyrone asked if I would buy popcorn when we watched it tomorrow. We usually watch it and score each country ourselves.

There was a separate programme on about the Eurovision song contest. Your group, The Brotherhood of Man, were on it like they are nearly every year and they showed them performing at the contest.

Watching them speaking and performing the song was a stark reminder of how heartbroken and troubled I became, I wanted you, Daddy, you were my Daddy that I adored, but ever since you remarried our relationship that we built up from when you abandoned me grew worse. She never liked my children or me and even stopped us from visiting you when you had your stroke.

Suddenly you appear in my mind, in one of your suits and smiling. As Tyrone your grandson said, your smile and presence lit up a whole room.

You won the Eurovision with the song, 'Save your Kisses for Me' but there will be **No more kisses for me,** and there haven't been any kisses for me, for a very long time. You left everything to her. You never even thought about me, your grandchildren or your great grandson, this is the ultimate betrayal, and through this grieving process, I have had to accept that you never really cared about us. They say that part of the grieving process is acceptance. I have finally at the expense of my emotional wellbeing realised that all those years I was in awe of Tony Hiller the successful Songwriter and not Tony Hiller the Daddy, that Tony Hiller never existed, only in my imagination.

She won't speak to me and the grandchildren, she has pulled up the drawbridge. Any decent woman who truly loved you, Daddy, surely would want us in her life to share the grief and memories that we all had, as we are the bloodline connection to you, but she has put the final nail in the coffin.

I have to live with the realisation for the rest of my life that you betrayed us all.

I'm done!! After you died and left me nothing, I realised that I had wasted years trying to get your love and affection back. You didn't care about me. You only wanted her to the expense of my heart, my feelings and my heartache that I had to go through every day of my life feeling rejected and that I wasn't good enough or smart enough. You try bringing three children up on a small budget. I was discarded like a rag doll. How does that make me feel? So sad. So bloody sad that it is tragic and then the resentment and anger set in.

I was staying in a house that was so old that a lick of paint never covered up the cracks. No matter what I did with a small budget, it was never enough.

I stayed at home day after day, night after night until my body and face resembled the cracks in the woodwork and floorboards. Well, now it is my time to get a life while I still have one.

I love you Daddy

RIP xxx

Letter 18: Closure

Dear Father,

This will be the very last letter that I will be writing to you. The previous letters I had written had been a catalyst to self-healing. You are probably wondering why I am now addressing you as father and not Daddy. Well, this is because time has passed and I have tried to make sense of our strained relationship. You were prevalent in my life from when I was small up to my early teens when you walked out. For a few years after that, we regained our relationship when you were around and not getting me to stay with family members because you were away working and touring with The Brotherhood of Man. You were my wonderful Daddy when you put me on your shoulders and played with me from an infant and gave me your time.

I want you to know that now I am so much stronger than I thought, and I have regained a lot of my self-confidence.

Time is a great healer but there are some things that impact our lives with such brute force that there will always be an indentation, a physical or mental scar but we as humans adapt and live with it.

You should be proud of me now. At this very moment as I am writing this letter, I am on my way to do an interview. You see, a literary agent was so interested in what I had written that I now have a publishing deal. Imagine that? People are praising me for my writing. From the start of the letters, I had poured out my heart to you from the depth of my soul. I loved you so much but ended up trying to get your attention for most of my life.

As a parent and grandmother myself I have had to accept that you made a new life and you and her didn't want me in it. It has been so hurtful for me to accept. It was wrong and I was completely justified in feeling the way I did for most of my life. It really didn't have to be like this at all. You and her lived in an insular bubble and nobody could enter that except for your showbiz friends and her friends that you paid so much attention to more than your own flesh and blood.

To be honest, in a strange way I am now replacing you as a writer, so it really doesn't matter that you never recognised my writing talents. I am now a published author, which is an achievement in itself. Let's be honest, there was only room for one successful person in the family and that was you.

People are actually treating me as an equal now and recognise my talent. I can't quite believe it and thought they were only doing it out of pity. How silly of me to think that but all those years of making me feel inadequate have had an effect on me.

Me and the family are still struggling financially but nothing new there. We have each other through good and bad times.

Mummy and Max are still helping out when needed and we will all have a lifetime of happy memories. Isn't that what family is all about?

She remains silent and still doesn't want to associate with us in any way. Your family still have this misplaced loyalty towards her. Me and the children are of no relevance or importance to them, but you did that. Are you proud of yourself? She was more important than us. I want you to know that we are all doing fine.

It's amusing to think that all those years ago, your sister said you and her lived in a bubble because in 2020 because of Covid, we are all living in bubbles of six and there is no room in our bubble for her.

She obviously doesn't have a conscience, which shows in the way she's always treated us, at arm's length in Life and in Death, that just says more about her than us. We dont care and It is time for closure and best to let it be. We are not responsible for other people's behaviour and I am not going to beat myself up about it as she has no relevance in our lives.

I wasn't going mad, and I wasn't this wild child you made me out to be, I was just being me and I have nothing to be ashamed of.

When you were alive, we were denied the right to spend time with you except for the monthly visits by appointment only. It appears this way even in death. We can't visit your grave as you were cremated. I thought it might be nice if me and the children visited your memorial plaque but after speaking to a woman at the crematorium, it appears that there is no memorial plaque of you. Apparently, your ashes were scattered there in the grounds and not on your parent's graves as was your last wish. It is as if you didn't exist.

I know for a fact there is a brighter future for me and my family. I am a someone. I won't ever let anyone make me feel that I am not good enough.

I dont want anyone else to feel the way I did or have to wait for another person's acceptance. The one thing I have learnt is that we must believe in ourselves and love ourselves. The only person we need approval from is indeed ourselves. It has taken me over two years since your death to believe in myself and the love and support of my cousin and her husband has helped me immensely. I started my journey through bereavement with them and I have ended up staying with them today. The day I have decided I need closure. What a coincidence or is it? There is a time for everything.

By writing these letters to you, I have realised that this is my own unique journey and I shouldn't have had to fight for your love or anyone else's. I can't ever take back those lost years that were filled with sadness. The emotional turmoil and unhappiness that enveloped me probably contributed towards my mental health issues but today I want closure. The sadness is still here but I now accept that is the way it was even though it was by no means right. I cannot continue going over it. I cannot punish myself anymore. There was no valid reason in you casting me aside while you and her were viewed as wonderful people. Look around, there are people who commit terrible acts and are still loved by their Parents. What the hell did I do? There was absolutely no justification in the way you looked down on my life and drip fed me parts of you and your time.

I like to remember you now as Tony Hiller who wrote the most successful Eurovision song contest winning song, Save your Kisses for Me.

R.I.P XX

About the Author

Born in London. Gayle had a happy childhood growing up in Chiswick. Her maternal grandparents lived upstairs in the maisonette. At the age of 9 her parents moved to Hadley common.

Her neighbours were Olivia Newton John and Bruce Welsh of the Shadows. At 13 her life was dramatically changed when a car smashed into her and flung her into the air at 30 miles per hour. Her body and skull smashed against an iron lamppost. In a coma and fighting for her life, Gayle had to learn to walk and write again. About a year later suffering mentally and physically from the accident, her Father Tony Hiller won The Eurovision song contest with the song, 'Save all your Kisses for me,' sang by the group, The Brotherhood of Man.

Her Father walked out on his family leaving her in great pain. After many attempts to see him she cut her wrists. Her life was vastly different, and she attended different schools. A very unhappy teenager she used to express herself writing poetry and short stories. She attended writers' workshops and poetry readings with her Aunt that she stayed with a lot.

Gayle has struggled with her mental health over the years and addiction to pills. When her Father died, she chose to take pills and curl up asleep on the settee. In trying to come to terms with her bereavement and all the hurt from her past, Gayle wrote letters to her

Father, things she couldnt tell him as she and her children could only see him every 4 to 6 weeks. He only cared about his new life with his second wife. Gayle tried to get back his love for years which caused her great distress.

One letter became 2, then 2 became 3 etc etc. Then it became a book. It is a very raw and emotional read.

About the Publisher

Two guys with extensive experience in publishing, editing, and SEO got together one afternoon and decided there were people out there with stories to tell but who needed help to bring them into the world. **Jerry Mooney** and **Troy Lambert** hammered the idea of helping others into establishing a publishing company that could offer innovative options and more than one path to publication for authors using modern technology, multimedia promotions, and the power of **print on demand** publishing.

Several months into the project, their company, **Unbound Publishing, LLC of Idaho** was contacted by **Rick Mayston** of **Agent Fox Media, London**. He proposed joining forces in a new venture to offer authors in the UK an alternative to the expense and risk of set print by applying the use of modern technology, multimedia promotions and multiple platforms **beyond the book**. These include gallery exhibitions, art, photos, music, and media appearances.

As a part of our partnership we are able to offer unique promotional opportunities including the **Agent Fox Media** YouTube program **"In the Fox's Den."** Not only is this a great media asset for authors, but it's shared across all social media platforms and distributed worldwide. This helps these great authors get the attention they deserve.

What started with a shared vision and a belief that authors deserve better brings us where we are today. The collaborative, post-Brexit, trans-Atlantic partnership formed in the middle of a global pandemic aims to give authors a voice, storytellers a chance to shine, and all under a hybrid, print on demand model that operates with a new kind of efficiency. **Print on demand** and modern tools enable us to produce products of the same or higher quality than publishers with set print runs are able to or willing to do. This makes books and media more profitable for both the publisher and the author.

The team includes **Rick and Beverley Mayston of Agent Fox Media, London**. **Jerry Mooney and Troy Lambert** are the co-founders of Unbound Publishing, LLC of Idaho, United States. We also thank our cover designer, **Mick Mamuzelos**, our editors **Dana Long and Jon Olsen**, proofreaders, formatters, and other members of both teams too countless to name here.

Want to keep up to date with what we are publishing next? Subscribe to our newsletter and check out the other books published under our partnership and published by **Unbound Publishing** by visiting our website, unboundpublish.com.

Are you a storyteller who wants to become an author? Your ideas, your story, could change the world, and we want to give you the best opportunity to do just that. Contact us today! If you're based in the UK, get in touch with **Rick** and **Agent Fox Media** at rick@agentfoxmedia.com and if you are in the US, email info@unboundpublish.com.

"Where storytellers become authors, and authors find the success they deserve."

Printed in Great Britain
by Amazon